VICTORIAN CRITICAL INTERVENTIONS
Donald E. Hall, Series Editor

VICTORIAN LESSONS
IN EMPATHY
AND DIFFERENCE

Rebecca N. Mitchell

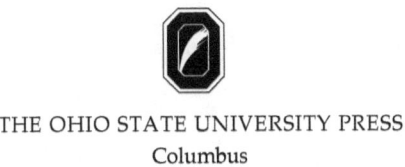

THE OHIO STATE UNIVERSITY PRESS
Columbus

Library of Congress Cataloging-in-Publication Data
Mitchell, Rebecca N. (Rebecca Nicole), 1976–
 Victorian lessons in empathy and difference / Rebecca N. Mitchell.
    p. cm. — (Victorian critical interventions)
 Includes bibliographical references and index.
 ISBN-13: 978-0-8142-1162-5 (cloth : alk. paper)
 ISBN-10: 0-8142-1162-3 (cloth : alk. paper)
 ISBN-13: 978-0-8142-9261-7 (cd)
 1. English literature—19th century—History and criticism. 2. Art, English—19th century. 3.
Other (Philosophy) in literature. 4. Other (Philosophy) in art. 5. Dickens, Charles, 1812–1870—
Criticism and interpretation. 6. Eliot, George, 1819–1880—Criticism and interpretation. 7.
Hardy, Thomas, 1840–1928—Criticism and interpretation. 8. Whistler, James McNeill, 1834–
1903—Criticism and interpretation. I. Title. II. Series: Victorian critical interventions.
 PR468.O76M58 2011
 820.9′008—dc22

                                    2011010005

This book is available in the following editions:
Cloth (ISBN 978-0-8142-1162-5)
CD-ROM (ISBN 978-0-8142-9261-7)

Cover design by Janna Thompson Chordas
Type set in Adobe Palatino

⊚ The paper used in this publication meets the minimum requirements of the American
National Standard for Information Sciences—Permanence of Paper for Printed Library Materials. ANSI Z39.48-1992.

9 8 7 6 5 4 3 2 1

CONTENTS

ILLUSTRATIONS

Figure 1

James McNeill Whistler, *The Miser* (1861). Drypoint on paper. Freer Gallery of Art, Smithsonian Institution, Washington, DC.: Gift of Charles Lang Freer, F1898.310. • 108

Figure 2

James McNeill Whistler, *Nocturne: Silver and Opal—Chelsea* (early 1880s). Oil on wood panel. Freer Gallery of Art, Smithsonian Institution, Washington, DC.: Gift of Charles Lang Freer, F1902.146a-b. • 109

Figure 3

James McNeill Whistler, *At the Piano* (1858–59). Oil on canvas. Bequest of Louise Taft Semple, Taft Museum of Art, Cincinnati, OH. Courtesy of the Taft Museum of Art, Cincinnati, OH. Photo Credit: Tony Walsh, Cincinnati, OH. • 110

Figure 4

James McNeill Whistler, *Harmony in Green and Rose: The Music Room* (1860–61). Oil on canvas. Freer Gallery of Art, Smithsonian Institution, Washington, DC.: Gift of Charles Lang Freer, F1917.234a-b. • 111

Figure 5

James McNeill Whistler, *Wapping* (1860–64). Oil on canvas. John J. Whitney Collection. Image courtesy National Gallery of Art, • 112

PREFACE

It is a common occurrence in the literature classroom: a student muses aloud that if only Pip would face the facts and get over Estella, or if Dorothea would realize the horrors that await her and refuse to marry Casaubon, or if Angel Clare would just forgive Tess's past transgressions—if characters in a novel would simply do something other than what they do—then they would avoid the painful events of the novel. Equally common, I imagine, is the professorial response: Pip is not real; Dorothea is not real; Angel is not real. These are not real people and they cannot choose to do something other than what is written on the page.

The tendency for students to relate to a novel's characters as real people, with real choices and real agency, seems painfully obvious to the practiced scholar. In order to facilitate students' attempts to analyze a text *as* a text, we must first break them of the comfortable habit of approaching texts as people.

And yet, aren't we so often guilty of the same? As easy as it is to spot the facile simplicity of the student who wonders why Jane Eyre doesn't just fix herself up—a dear friend vividly remembers when, as an undergraduate herself, a fellow student asked that very question in a Victorian literature course, to which the frustrated professor responded in a tone of woe-tinged anger, "Jane Eyre had no hair!"—we fail to recognize the tendency of criticism, especially ethical criticism, to relate to novelistic characters exactly as if they were people. And not simply any people, but people who can teach us important lessons, encourage us to altruistic behavior, and provide cautionary examples of how not to behave; think of Wayne Booth's description of that "unique value of fiction": "its relatively cost-free offer of trial runs."[1] We insist that our students are wrong, that the characters in novels are not people; yet what ethical argument does not depend on their functioning precisely as other humans?

On a fundamental level, it seems that to deny characters human attributes is to foreclose the possibility of ethical growth. If we cannot relate to the novel or its subjects on a human level, how might we learn the human lessons the novel offers? George Eliot's famous formulation—that art must "enlarge men's sympathies"—depends on characters standing in for people, functioning for the reader in place of the "others" they may not otherwise come across, doesn't it?

In this book, I argue that Victorian novels and paintings work hard to disabuse their readers and viewers of this tendency. They do so on two levels: first, they depict the *unknowability* of the human other. There are distinct limits to knowledge, and the ultimate limit case in the realist work is the human being. Second, these works insist on the distinction—in both form and content—between that unknowability of the person and the knowability of art. Stories can be learned, novels are finite; people, however, are not. These texts and images thus inscribe alterity through their representation of human interaction, and they enact the absence of alterity through their very substance. A reader can know a book, and can know a painting, but the subjects of those books and paintings can never fully know each other.

I do not disagree with the idea that novels teach us how to empathize. Indeed they do. But in this book, I suggest a radical revision of the mode through which that ethical expansion takes place. Art can edify its audience, but we have failed to recognize one mechanism of that edification. Realist art does not make empathy possible by teaching readers what it is like to be another person; it makes empathy possible by teaching us that the alienation that exists between the self and the other cannot be fully overcome, that the alterity of the human other is infinite and permanent. But in that radical, inalterable alterity exists the possibility of ethical engagement.

Perhaps this formulation seems ungenerous. It is human nature to want to overcome a sense of alienation; we want to think that through hard work, we may reach a state of identification leading to sympathy or, better yet, empathy. We have been told for centuries, perhaps most influentially by Adam Smith, that this is how fellow feeling arises. Novels, under that schema, can teach us how to empathize by moving readers through a series of paces: setting up an unfamiliar character who becomes known, possibly endearing, potentially lovable, through the exposure gained by the time and effort required to read the text. This desire explains why a common analogy—that a character in a book, or even a book itself, is like a person—is so very compelling. The complete knowledge we can have of a novel's characters fills up the void that must necessarily exist in human interactions. That analogy elides an important distinction, however, between character and person: a character is—*to the reader*—finite and knowable, but a person is—*to another person*—ultimately unknowable. And so a novel may depict the realization of alterity between characters, but the same realization cannot exist between a reader and a character.

Part of what I'm saying may seem familiar—others have gestured toward the very limitation that my book is built upon: we cannot know people, but we can know the people in books. E. M. Forster describes this condition with such clarity and precision that his formulation deserves to be quoted:

> For human intercourse, as soon as we look at it for its own sake and not as a social adjunct, is seen to be haunted by a spectre. We cannot understand each other, except in a rough and ready way; we cannot reveal ourselves, even when we want to; what we call intimacy is only a makeshift; perfect knowledge is an illusion. But in the novel we can know people perfectly, and, apart from the general pleasure of reading, we can find here a compensation for their dimness in life. . . . They are people whose secret lives are visible or might be visible: we are people whose secret lives are invisible.
>
> And that is why novels, even when they are about wicked people, can solace us; they suggest a more comprehensible and thus a more manageable human race, they give us the illusion of perspicacity and of power.[2]

What makes a character in a novel realistic, in Forster's telling, is in fact antithetical to what makes human beings human: a character in a book is real, he writes, "when the novelist knows everything about it," even if the novelist withholds some of that "everything" from the page.[3] That his argument, so clearly rendered, did not forestall decades of ethical criticism insisting on ideas contrary to his demonstrates the concentrated power of the solace he describes. I want to insist steadfastly that to the reader, a novel's characters are knowable. Only to the other characters *within* the work are fictional people "others."

Realist novels depict characters who recognize on some level the ultimate unknowability of another character, and more often they depict those who plow ahead assuming (erroneously) that in fact they do know exactly what the other is thinking and who the other is. Such is the marvelous faculty of the omniscient narrator or the multiplot structure that those formal qualities of the book can lay bare the gulf of alterity to the reader, even though the characters within may remain ignorant. Tertius Lydgate might think he knows Rosamond Vincy, but we readers know better.

There are two levels of knowledge, then, presented by these works: the limited knowledge shared by the subjects of art, and the comprehensive knowledge available to the audience. Where we (the audience) get muddled—to borrow Forster's word—is in the confusing of the two. The lesson of Victorian realism is that we *cannot* know the other, and since that lesson applies only to the human other, the means of pedagogy— the book, the painting—must be safe from presumptions of alterity. But the impulse to view artworks as analogous to people is strong, as is our belief that identifying with or knowing the other is essential to empathic or ethical extension. To counter the strength of that desire, I call upon the work of Emmanuel Levinas, who gives language to the idea that acknowledging alterity, and not overcoming it, is ethics. His phenomenology reframes the apperception of alterity not as an obstacle but rather as the very means to interpersonal ethics. Essential to Levinas's formulation is the denial of the book-to-person analogy, as any work of art is fungible and ultimately knowable.

It is indeed problematic for humans living together to treat other people as if they were books: knowable, fungible. But for the literary critic, at least, and I would argue for any engaged reader, the inverse of the analogy is equally troublesome. When we treat artworks as human— when we insist that the art object can and should function as the other— we miss the point that these works are at pains to make. We can know the subjects of art precisely because they are subjects of art. The nonhuman-ness of the novel or painting is what gives us the tantalizing feeling that we have access to a person in a way that, in reality, we lack.

ACKNOWLEDGMENTS

I couldn't have written this book without the support and insight of my friends and colleagues. Crisillia Benford, Danika Brown, Danielle Coriale, Marty Gould, Anna Maria Jones, and Maggie Sloan de Lloret were inexhaustible sources of encouragement and patient readers of my work. Susan Derwin and Kay Young were, and are, extraordinary mentors. For their unflagging support and friendship, I also thank Ljiljana Coklin, Aimee Kilbane, Marci McMahon, Caroline Miles, Anna Tillett, and Stacey van Dahm. To my family, especially Gloria Tobey and Matt Kuss, I owe more than I can express.

I am grateful to the editors and readers at The Ohio State University Press for their patient support of this project and their invaluable feedback.

The University of Texas-Pan American provided grants that supported my research for this book; Ala Qubbaj, in particular, was an outstanding advocate of my project. I thank my colleagues in the English department—especially Gary Schneider, Matt Christensen, Melynda Nuss, David Anshen, and Shawn Thomson—who made it a pleasure to work among a community of scholars. Thanks also to Pamela Anderson-Mejías and Steven Schneider.

My work at the Freer Gallery wouldn't have been possible without the gracious help of Tim Kirk and Christina Popenfus. The Freer generously allowed me to reproduce the Whistler images from their collections.

An early version of part of the second chapter appeared as "Learning to Read: Interpersonal Literacy in *Adam Bede*" in *Papers on Language and Literature* volume 44, number 2, from spring 2008 (Copyright © 2008 by The Board of Trustees, Southern Illinois University). It is reprinted with their permission, for which I am grateful.

Alterity and the Limits of Realism

We made a pause at the toy shop in Fleet Street, to see the giants of Saint Dun-
stan's strike upon the bells—we had timed our going, so as to catch them at it, at
twelve o'clock—and then went on towards Ludgate Hill, and St. Paul's Church-
yard. We were crossing to the former place, when I found that my aunt greatly
accelerated her speed, and looked frightened. I observed, at the same time, that a
lowering ill-dressed man who had stopped and stared at us in passing, a little
before, was coming so close after us as to brush against her.

"Trot! My dear Trot!" cried my aunt, in a terrified whisper, and pressing my
arm. "I don't know what I am to do."

"Don't be alarmed," said I. "There's nothing to be afraid of. Step into a shop,
and I'll soon get rid of this fellow."

"No, no, child!" she returned. "Don't speak to him for the world. I entreat, I
order you!"

"Good Heaven, aunt!" said I. "He is nothing but a sturdy beggar."

"You don't know what he is!" replied my aunt. "You don't know who he is!
You don't know what you say!"

—*Charles Dickens,* David Copperfield[1]

The above scene is not pivotal in the plot of *David Copperfield*, but it illustrates a quiet dynamic which rules that plot: the realization that one's knowledge of another—even family members or dear friends—is incomplete at best. Copperfield's aunt is known by her family as Miss Betsey, and long before David meets her, arriving unannounced on her doorstep after abandoning his miserable London existence, he knows her through stories told by his mother. Miss Betsey's storied past mingles with David's years-long experience living with her, resulting in the closest familial relationship David has; he even takes her name. At Ludgate Hill on a shopping day, David is thus shocked to learn that his dear Aunt Betsey Trotwood, whom he loves and has known better than nearly anyone else in his life, is in this moment a stranger to him. The man who Copperfield assumes is a "nothing but sturdy beggar" is in fact much more than that. He is the husband of Miss Betsey Trotwood, long believed to be dead, and his revelation throws into question, at least briefly, even Betsey's title; she is no longer "Miss," is she? Betsey herself abandons her usual self-command in favor of near-hysterics, a response that David cannot comprehend, and though she begins by articulating her own uncertainty—"I do not know what I am to do"—she ends by transferring uncertainty to David. By repeating "you do not know," Betsey underscores David's lack of comprehension. This scene, and Miss Betsey's insistent exclamations, illustrate a realization essential to realist representation: the human embodies the unknown.

Miss Betsey Trotwood's admonition to her young nephew speaks to a condition larger than the immediate moment on Ludgate Hill. In this book, I take up the mantle of Miss Betsey Trotwood's reproach—"you do not know"—to argue that realist texts and images embrace the inherent limitations of the unknowable other. As depicted in *David Copperfield*, confronting the real alterity of another person can, paradoxically, lead to an enhanced sense of that individual. We cannot fully know the other. That the idea can be so simply stated might suggest that the idea can be simply learned, but nothing could be further from the truth. Realist novels and paintings of the nineteenth century demonstrate that moving into the recognition of alterity is a process through which one comes to realize one's limits. To attain what these texts conceive as literacy is to learn that empathetic extension arises from the recognition of difference. I suggest that realists illustrate the problems that result when one individual does not or cannot recognize the difference between herself and others, because that failure overlooks the limitations of knowledge. In these instances, empathic extension occurs only through the appreciation of the limits of the self. These works demonstrate that effective connection between people is predicated on the recognition of such very limits. Novels employ strategies of reading to present a means of engaging alterity; paintings employ strategies of seeing to do the same. Realism thus points to the unknowable in addition to describing the knowable world.

The works addressed in this study—by Dickens, George Eliot, Thomas Hardy, and J. M. Whistler, among others—not only depict humans in community as ultimately unknowable and inscrutable but also engage the ethical imperative that arises from interaction with the unknowable other, an ethics that, in the twentieth century, Emmanuel Levinas defined in terms of alterity. As depicted in these works, recognition of this alterity is not easily achieved, not inherent in human interactions, but rather must be learned. Realist novels and paintings show individuals growing into this recognition by learning to appreciate difference: a character, for example, might realize an empathic relationship only after the often difficult process of setting another character free from her preconceived ideas or self-centered readings. Realist texts and images further insist through both form and content that while an artwork may represent the process of apprehending the alterity of the other, it cannot provide the reader or viewer a means of achieving that process. The novel and the painting, in other words, cannot function as "other" for the viewer or reader.

J. M. W. Turner and the Representation of Difference

You will find no better teachers than your own eyes, if used aright to see things as they are.
   —J. M. W. Turner, to students at the Royal Academy[2]

I have so far elided the distinction between textual and visual literacy, but the characteristics of visual literacy make it a particularly useful entrée into issues of interpretation and comprehension. Joseph Mallord William Turner's oeuvre, spanning from the end of the eighteenth century until the middle of the nineteenth, can frame the shift toward the foregrounding of uncertainty that fully develops later in the century. His work suggests that realist depiction of limitation is not new, but rather had been percolating for some time. Turner's instruction to his students at the Royal Academy offers both a lucid declaration of a primary tenet of art in the nineteenth century and an indication of the murky boundaries of that tenet: "paint what you see," he seems to say, but the advice is tempered by one condition—that the eyes are used "aright." To paint the reality one sees, one must be taught to see as much as one is taught to paint. And being taught to see is as much learning to appreciate what is before our eyes as learning to recognize what is beyond the limits of our perception. Turner's style, with its divergence from the then normative representational strategies used by other artists, inscribes difficulty into the viewing process, complicating the easy approach of reading meaning, if not an explicit narrative, into an image. Instead, Turner's paintings demand that their viewers encounter them as surface and not as narrative. That proto-realist insistence fuels my approach to the novel; Turner's example makes the case for viewing text as painting, not painting as text.

Turner's art, with its idiosyncratic renderings of sunsets and fogs, made the common world of England appear new to those who had seen its landscapes and natural effects throughout their daily lives. Such newness was not always appreciated by the viewing public, however, and his works were met with ambivalence throughout his active career. While Turner's *The Fighting Temeraire* received at first a merely "sympathetic reception,"[3] by 2006 the painting was voted the "Greatest Painting in Britain" by the British public.[4] Ezra Pound understood that Turner's paintings could *only* have been misconstrued upon first exhibition. He noted that Turner's pictures "educated up" their viewers: standing in front of his paintings one might be perplexed, "but when you leave the pictures you see beauty in mists, shadows, a hundred places where you never dreamed of seeing it before."[5] Without being overtly pedantic, Turner developed a pictorial vocabulary that enriched the visual literacy of his audience; his works "taught" their viewers. Pound's comment was itself not particularly novel in 1909, and Viktor Shklovsky and the Russian Formalists would later tease the idea into the literary application of "defamiliarization." What Turner did in images in the early part of the nineteenth century was precisely to render the familiar unfamiliar, changing the public's vision as well as conventions of the medium. A similar effect was achieved by realist authors; note Erich Auerbach's praise of Zola's novels, which echoes a Turneresque emphasis on visual literacy: "Did anyone," he asks, "before [Zola] see a tenement house as he did in the second chapter of *L'Assommoir*? Hardly!"[6] The question is not one of sight, but one of vision. And by focusing their vision on stories not told, images not painted, and characters not represented, realists built upon Turner's example (not only depicting difference but emphasizing it) and ushered in a new artistic vocabulary. That their public or critics would uniformly understand it, or even welcome it, was perhaps too much to expect.

Given the significant overlap in the representational strategies employed in both realist texts and images, it is not surprising that critics responded similarly to both media.[7] Yet there is a danger in collapsing entirely the difference in apprehending images and texts. First, by imagining the apparatus of texts and images as being inherently the same, many tend either to narrativize every image or regard the image merely as a portal composed of symbols to be interpreted.[8] Second, doing so can result in problematizing verisimilitude in images more than is necessary. The overlap between style—the conventions of visual rendering—and a sense of reality in painting (especially) has had an unmistakably strong foundation throughout Western history of the development of the medium. Verisimilitude has been at stake at least since Zeuxis challenged Parhassius.[9] And that each successive generation of artists sought to improve upon the veridicality of the previous generation is also a saw of art-historical surveys—the trick was, the argument goes, the development of technologies of representation and the viewing public's ability to process and accept those technologies as being *more* representative of perceived reality than what came before.[10] The movement toward greater verisimilitude seems to suggest that we're moving ever closer to the depiction of things as they really are, and along with greater lifelikeness, greater recognition and therefore greater knowledge will ensue. Turner offers an early example that greater verisimilitude can foreground visual uncertainty, and in fact decrease familiarity. It is almost as if an actual correlation between representation and "the real" in painting is bracketed; this sensation is particularly evident when reading psychologically inflected histories of art such as Gombrich's seminal *Art and Illusion,* in which he convincingly adopts a formalist reading of the seemingly teleological march of the visual arts toward illusionistic verisimilitude. One benefit of such bracketing and the formalist readings that result is an emphasis on the surface, the artifice, and the conventions of the visual arts.

In light of those conventions, novelistic claims of truth might seem quaint in their earnestness, as authors did what painters rarely did—they included *within* their works claims of veracity.[11] The concreteness of those claims (as opposed to the effusive, implicit nature of Turner's sunsets, for example) opens the texts to criticism based on fidelity to intention: are the authors able to meet the standards they propose, standards that seem impossibly extreme? An impossible aim coupled with content focusing on people and places hitherto underrepresented in fiction, including the rural, the poor, the laboring, and the common— these aspects of the movement open literary realists to critique. Claims of truth become naturalized, as if engagement with realist texts ought to be easy rather than difficult. If what's being represented is reality, we should be able to recognize it immediately; it should remind us of ourselves and our world. But problems arise if the reality represented is the impossibility of representation, the limits of knowledge. That assumption underpins much critical reaction to realist novels, which is hyperfocused on the differences between realist conventions or content and that of non-realist works, to the extent that it fails to recognize that the novels themselves describe and depict the recognition of difference and, more important, the limitations of knowledge. The insistence on object-ness embodied in Turner's work provides a counterpoint to those critical gestures, if only his lessons can be retained.

"Defective" Mirrors: Realist Claims and Critical Responses

The nineteenth century dislike of Realism is the rage of Caliban seeing his own face in a glass.

—*Oscar Wilde*, The Picture of Dorian Gray[12]

In his 1891 preface to *The Picture of Dorian Gray*, Oscar Wilde's aphoristic take on realism is partnered with his similarly glib (or genially sincere) take on Romanticism: "the rage of Caliban not seeing his own face in a glass." Wilde identifies both literary movements as provoking "dislike" among their readership, especially their critical readership. That dislike is essential to understanding how the critical response frames the discussion of realism's successes and failures, just as the mechanisms of realist critique are essential to understanding the role that difference plays in the realist project. Moreover, Wilde's epigrams demonstrate the ambivalence that is at the heart of so much criticism of realism, namely the pressing desire to see oneself reflected accurately and the repulsion at seeing in that reflection an unfamiliar vision of oneself or one's world.

Wilde's invocation of the mirror in both descriptions presents as a given one principle of artistic production that is disputable, for he seems to accept that realist or Romantic art can function as a mirror. In fact, the *inability* of art to reflect reality accurately has always been a part of the realist impulse, at least from the perspective of the artist. Claims of exact verisimilitude come more often from critics. The loud, reductive voice of the most vociferous criticism persists long after the more subtle, nuanced modulations of the artists themselves, and critical responses to realism lay bare some of the primary anxieties pervading its readership, concerns that continue to guide our present conceptualization and analysis of the genre. To be sure, the anger at seeing one's true self reflected in art noted by Wilde can certainly account for some, but not all, of the vituperative responses to realism. Seeing the *other* defamiliarized, through representations that break free from existent artistic conventions and readerly expectations,[13] was equally provocative. Early responses to realism included a mix of reactions to seeing the self and seeing the radically other, manifested in twin objections to form and to content.

The most persistent charge against realist fiction is an assault on its perceived claim of veracity, a charge that establishes a dangerous series of mutually exclusive potentialities, starting with the most basic: truth or falsity. J. Hillis Miller summarized the problem with a battery of binary constructions; criticism of realism, he writes, "tends to express itself in either/or dichotomies: either realism or vacuous, free-floating fiction; [. . .] either the representation of some verifiable and objective truth, or merely the relative, some partial, subjective truth, therefore no truth at all."[14] *Any* indication of deviance from a purely objective truth thus rendered the whole effort futile. Indeed, early iterations of realism did seem to support such all-or-nothing paradigms, as they regularly employed superlative language. The earliest definitions of the term came out of France, and between 1841 and 1851 French critics of art and literature characterized realism as follows: "the exact imitation of nature just as she is" (Gautier); "nature herself as she is, without lying and without ornamentation" (Houssaye); "the great merit of seeing and rendering nature, just as it is" (Clément de Ris); "the faithful reproduction of the first passing object" (Geofroy); and "[the] claim that all, ugly and ignoble, can and must be represented under the single condition that the imitation be faithful" (Delécluze).[15] Lofty ideals, to be sure. These definitions also do not address how realist goals differ from those of any other literary movement, which aspects of nature realist artists choose to replicate faithfully, or with what formal characteristics they do so, demonstrating a lack of precision that was itself regarded as anathema to realism's very goals.

Such critiques persist to this day, as can be seen in the ongoing debates on epistemology and representation in realist fiction. George Levine's introduction to *Realism and Representation* (1993) presents the then current status of the debate, termed in largely stark distinctions similar to those articulated by J. Hillis Miller: realist versus antirealist, positivist versus relativist, and so forth. After noting the violent responses of academics against the very idea of "objectivity," Levine summarizes: "The views that all facts are theory laden, that all argument is 'interested,' that all knowledge is culturally constructed, that all reality is mediated by representation, are dominant in literary theory and criticism, in sociology of science, and in some areas of the philosophy of science. The exposure of the hidden political, social, and gender implications of 'facts' and 'objectivity' and rigorous procedures of verification has been one of the most exciting and valuable activities of modern intellectuals," before warning that, taken to the extreme, such skepticism leads to "relativism and [. . .] anti-intellectualism."[16] Just as the "exposure" of fissures in the ideas of "truth" or "objectivity" may lead to relativism or anti-intellectualism, those same critiques have also led to a wholesale condemnation of the realist project; as described in J. Hillis Miller's account, rigid binaries can result in the "realist" baby being thrown out with the "subjective" bathwater. Critic Michael Boyd, for example, decries realism for "[pretending] to be what it is not" and declares it "a form of bad faith" because realist authors "pretend that their art is not a compromise but a slice of life—not the whole of life, perhaps, but a selection that reveals a one-to-one relationship with the experience to which it refers."[17] D. A. Williams similarly speaks of the realist's choice of content as a resignation to what cannot possibly be: "Knowing the dream of total absorption of the real to be impossible, the realist resigns himself to working with a scaled-down model of reality."[18]

These objections depend on a definition of realism more akin to that of the French critics than that of the artists themselves. Realists repeatedly address another central issue that is raised in Wilde's quip: the trustworthiness of the mirror. The "glass" is a metaphor used consistently by realists to describe their work, but those metaphors often hedge the very meaning of the term by limiting or restricting the mirror's accuracy. For Balzac the mirror was but "some sort" of "concentric" mirror (his inability to articulate precisely what that meant is clear in the original French: the artist *est obligé d'avoir en lui je ne sais quel miroir concentrique où, suivant sa fantaisie, l'univers vient se réfléchir"*),[19] and for Eliot the mirror was doubtlessly "defective" and the reflections "faint or confused."[20] Allowing that even a mirror might be affected by the experience of the individual acknowledges the difficulty of transcending one's own subjectivity, a proposition that is echoed in constructions that do not depend on the mirror as a symbol. Zola describes art not as a reproduction of nature but as the representation of objects being filtered through the screen of the artist's temperament.[21] Dickens, in the preface to *Oliver Twist*, mitigates his promise to "paint" the criminals of London "in all their deformity, in all their wretchedness, in all the squalid misery of their lives; to show them as they really were" by noting that he performed the task "as best I could."[22]

In spite of such admissions, the critical eye often regards limitation as a deciding factor in the zero-sum game of truth, which results in criticism dependent on the objective/subjective binary. According to Lillian Furst, the mirror's status as "the symbol of realism" only calls attention to the "pretense that [realism] tries to maintain." She continues:

Far from the anonymous, unbiased, scientific instrument that it was meant to be, the mirror acts as a prism in its passage through the artist's evaluating mind. It offers, therefore, not a faithful, objective replica of actuality as it "really" is, but a subjective interpretation of things as they seem through the refraction of the perceiving mind.[23]

Realists seem not only to admit but to promote this more limited vision of their powers. The charge of "bad faith" must then be considered in light of the literary critics who make the charges, whose own weighted assessments affect their readings. Such critics hold claims of comprehensive objectivity up to stronger scrutiny than any acknowledgment (whether within or without a literary work) that an attempt to comprehensiveness is inherently and unavoidably limited. Interpreters of texts are naturally limited by our *own* cultural context, our own limitations. And while today we critique the realists' implicit dependence on hegemonic structures to present a supposedly single, privileged, and therefore problematic version of reality, in the authors' own time the charge would more likely have been that they were in fact violating the standards of the hegemonic order.

The vituperative cast of much contemporary criticism of realism suggests that the claim of objective representation was, at the time, less challenged than was the artists' choice of content: assuming the mirror is to any extent accurate, why choose to represent Caliban instead of Miranda; why choose to depict the ugly instead of the beautiful? Claims of truth and dispassionate representation were collapsed by readers with visions of familiarity: *the* truth was understood to be *my* truth. If the subject choices were unfamiliar to the reader, or were outside of the bounds of acceptability (conditions that often overlapped), the creative agent was seen as culpable. Consider the heated British response to Émile Zola's fiction. Claiming to depict the real, Zola was charged instead with opting for a more violent, negatively skewed version of life. If this was reality, the British did not like "seeing it in a glass" at all. According to *The Globe*, Zola's works "sapped the foundations of manhood and womanhood, not only destroyed innocence, but corroded the moral nature," and the Birmingham *Daily Mail* asserted that the author himself "simply wallowed in immorality."[24] In charging Zola's publisher with immorality for publishing *Nana, La Terre* (a novel that won Zola the decoration of the Legion of Honor in France), and *Pot-Bouille,* the court declared they were "the three most immoral books ever published!"[25] Their immorality arose not because the novels were false or deceitful, but rather because their author *chose* to represent in text realities that were deemed offensive and because their publisher *chose* to publish them.

If the mirror is regarded as accurate and the reflection as complete, the public objects to what is reflected. If, even as Balzac and Eliot note, the mirror must necessarily be warped or clouded, then the objections raised are that the reflection is inaccurate. Representation is thus placed in a bind; one escape from that bind is to depict the limitations or the defects of the reflection accurately (a proposal that gives rise to the Barthian construction of realism as a textual strategy that makes its artifice clearly evident[26]) and to represent the limits of representation.

Responding to Difference: Detachment versus Self-Extension

> *I aspire to give no more than a faithful account of men and things as they have mirrored themselves in my mind.*
>
> —*George Eliot*, Adam Bede[27]

Critical responses both to content and to form demonstrate reactions to difference, either a text appearing different from its stated goal or its content appearing different from the expected. Further, each objection is founded on an assumption: in the first case that an objective point of view is possible and or representative of reality, and in the second case that the acceptable real is somehow aligned with the pleasant or the moral. Overcoming these assumptions is necessary to understanding how realism represents the human other as a limit case of knowledge without falling into bad faith; it is useful to articulate the realist project in terms that emphasize its drive toward an ideal rather than its success or failure at achieving that ideal.

Novels and paintings of the period depict the difference of the sovereign other from oneself, engage that difference, and replicate the alienation felt in an encounter with such difference. Most importantly, they show that overcoming alienation is an impossibility. This bears repeating: elemental to the moral claims that underpin realism is the recognition that alterity cannot be overcome. A most important means of addressing difference is via representations of failure, especially the failure to achieve an ultimate objectivity. As discussed above, realists entertain the mirror's failure as a foundational truth of their work, and not as an impediment. Ameliorating the potential negative effects of depictions of the pedestrian or base subject is made possible in part via this narratorial distance, born not of bad faith but of an acceptance that limitations are inherently part of the human lived experience. It is an ambivalent position, to be sure, but such distance allows for a movement toward a critical, detached understanding of even oneself, and certainly others.

Current criticism attempts to understand or theorize those realist encounters with difference, and one more nuanced way to approach realist works is by recognizing their rendering or installation of what Amanda Anderson refers to as "detachment"—a complex balance of acknowledging difference or distinction while not employing distance as a means to dismiss, wholesale, the other.[28] Anderson's analysis provides a useful model for my study because it embraces ambivalence and interminability as being constructive aspects of detachment. Detachment is thus not necessarily a final stance, but is instead a process that takes as its aim the possibility of an objective consideration of the "facets of human existence so as to better understand, criticize, and at times transform them."[29] The movement toward objectivity is not to be confused with objectivity itself, and Anderson is clear to note that the cultivation of detachments is an "*aspiration* to a distanced view" as opposed to an absolute objectivity that cannot be achieved.[30] This "distanced view" is explicitly not superlative or extreme, a distinction imperative to understanding Victorian realism. If Eliot, for example, argues for a disinterested perspective for her readers and characters, she also acknowledges the risks of wholesale detachment: in "German Life" she warns of the potential for regarding all country hay-balers as jolly, happy, rosy-cheeked people.[31]

My interest is in the singularity of otherness found expressly in the closeness of familial or communal relationships, relationships that sit outside of the binary systems long ascribed to realism and elucidated above whereby the "other" gets placed in a dialectic relationship with the self. It is easy to understand otherness in terms of the seemingly radical other, differentiated by nationality, class, race, or gender, while necessarily overlooking the fact that those who look much like oneself must in fact be understood as radically other as well. The binary formulation lulls one into thinking that if the other doesn't appear to be wholly other, she must be just like me. This sensibility is not born of critics but was, as Tim Barringer writes, a paradigm through which the Victorians "defined" themselves: "Respectable society in Victorian Britain defined itself through a series of structured oppositions by which any group thought to adhere to different concepts of social and sexual behavior, of work and time discipline, of value and of religion, was accorded the status of an inferior and potentially hostile other."[32] Barringer, in his study of the pictorial representation of difference, posits race as the "most powerful" of these factors of otherness. As Barringer notes, racial difference was regarded as being easily represented and thus easily perceived. If, as he suggests, "the field of visual representation offered a site for the production and dramatization of powerful distinctions between self and others," those who are unlike oneself are "constructed as deviant," while those who appear to be like oneself are understood in terms of that similarity.[33]

While not dismissing the distant or foreign other—whether they be the rural poor or those colonized across an ocean[34]—I wish to focus on the intimate interpersonal relationships that, in spite of or perhaps because of their banality, populate realist works. It is those closest relationships that abound in Victorian texts and paintings, and which prove most difficult to navigate, in large part because intimacy itself (even proximity itself) obstructs one's realization of the other's alterity, despite the necessity of that realization. In this way, the interpersonal relationships depicted in realist works echo the inherent closeness, the connection between what is depicted in realist works and what one sees in the real world. Achieving a critical distance becomes difficult for readers, even if it is encouraged by the writers and painters. As Kay Young writes, "The experience of intersubjectivity—knowing another and being known by another—depends on the acknowledgment of separate and mutual presence, or experiencing one's own separate presence in simultaneity with the other's separate, co-presence."[35] Thinking outside of the self seems necessary to sharing an intersubjective experience, and thus in addition to knowing the other better, one comes to know oneself better.

It is an idea that already had currency in the nineteenth century. John Stuart Mill, for example, asserted that failing to know the other can only lead to failing to know the self. Mill reminds us that what we believe may be false; those who "have never thrown themselves into the mental position of those who think differently" may not, "in any proper sense of the word, know the doctrine which they themselves profess."[36] The rub is that Mill's reading of detachment persists in placing the self in relation to the other and is fraught (as Anderson admits) with susceptibility to the same critiques of hegemonic power relationships that are leveled at realism itself: there is no pure detachment just as there can be no pure objectivity. Emmanuel Levinas, as will become clear, escapes this bind by removing any definition of the self from a dependent relationship with the other. For him, the other's alterity does not determine the self, just as

Anderson's reading hinges on the claim of *aspiration* toward detachment as opposed to an achievement of complete detachment.

George Levine's *Dying to Know* takes up this paradigm of aspiration to consider the intersection of scientific epistemology and ethics: "in the nineteenth century," he writes, "despite overt attempts to separate" the two, "the epistemological was latent with ethical force."[37] In Levine's telling, scientific inquiry requires dispassion, but the force driving the inquiry must be passionate, and the ethical is necessarily bound up in that drive. "Can those self-interested organisms usually identified through the hermeneutics of suspicion, in fact act in the interest of others at the possible sacrifice of themselves?" he asks. "To deny the possibility of objectivity, the capacity to be in that nowhere from which truth at last will be visible, is, logically speaking, to deny the possibility of altruism."[38] It is a sentiment echoed in another aspirational model of Victorian narrative—the form that Andrew Miller terms "moral perfectionism."[39] These analyses of Victorian works demonstrate that accounting for altruism within the realist text is, even in its most simple incarnation, a complicated endeavor.

Levine's description harkens to Anderson's "detachment," as he notes that the writers he addresses find "that some mode of detachment, some way to move beyond the personal and to recognize a responsibility to community and to knowledge, is essential both to the work of knowing and to the work of living meaningfully."[40] Anderson accounts for this responsibility by describing always the "aspiration" to detachment, rather than working out whether it is even possible, while Levine frames the problem by constantly questioning the absolute. To be sure, the work of much postmodern and critical theory asserts that there is no such absolute. But Levine, echoing his introduction to *Realism and Representation*, points out that such critiques are themselves totalizing. Within these critiques, questions of power and hegemony arise. That is, because power is at play, definitive pronouncements about the nature of realism, or the truth, are generally created by and in favor of those controlling the power.

Anderson and Levine thus describe the realist project in terms that emphasize its drive toward an inevitable impossibility: the aspiration to detachment or to an epistemological perspective that depends on objectivity. Yet their accounts do not present realism as a failed project. Realism demonstrates its inherent limitations through depiction; this is a constructive, even necessary component of its aesthetics and form, and not a negation of its goal that can only be understood as a pretense or as exhibiting bad faith. For Eliot to consider this process of representation as the "raw material of moral sentiment" does not do away with Levine's claim that true objectivity would eliminate the potential for true altruism.

I argue that realist works depict both elements of the complicated relationship between detachment and an ethics: realization of the radical alterity of the individual is necessary because in its absence, relationships fail, misunderstandings abound, or communities fracture. The other is beyond the conception of the self, is the ultimate unknowable, and the limit case of objective rendering for an author or painter, for the other *cannot* be rendered completely. And yet if one can appreciate the fundamental difference between the self and the other, if one can aspire to an escape from solipsism and set even an idea of the other free from the bounds of that solipsism, the result can be rife with potential for positive (or negative) affective possibilities. Escape from solipsism arises not from the belief that one understands the other, but rather that one ultimately cannot know what it really is to be the other. It is a movement toward an understanding of the other completely outside of the self. It requires an empathic extension born of detachment.

This formulation requires a departure from descriptions of self-extension, whether called sympathy or empathy, that involve the merging of the self and the other—this merging is common in criticism of Victorian literature.[41] Audrey Jaffe describes sympathy as an undoing of the recognition of alterity, describing Victorian scenes evoking sympathy as those that involve a "spectator's (dread) fantasy of occupying another's social place."[42] And if this fantasy can—should—be used to altruistic ends, it can offer an "affective solution to the problem of class alienation," and can "ameliorate social differences with assurances of mutual feeling and universal humanity."[43] This version follows on the heels of the predominant eighteenth-century notion of sympathy articulated by David Hume and Adam Smith, and described by David Marshall as "experiences of compassion, commiseration, pity, and identification."[44] Such sympathy is expressly predicated upon identification with another. Hume conceived of sympathy as a means to uniting people through fellow feeling; because "the minds of men are mirrors to one another,"[45] through mirroring the other, one can come to knowledge of that other. Adam Smith's description of the process of sympathy opens up some room for the distinction between the self and other, though ultimately he maintains the solipsism of the sympathizer that characterizes Hume's descriptions. In the opening of Smith's *The Theory of Moral Sentiments*, he writes, "As we have no immediate experience of what other men feel, we can form no idea of the manner in which they are affected, but by conceiving what we ourselves should feel in the like situation."[46] Here Smith acknowledges the untraversable gulf between the self and the other, and since our senses "never did, and never can, carry us beyond our own person," if we are to experience what the other experiences, we must rely on our imagination. "It is the impressions of our own senses only," Smith concedes, "not those of [the other], which our imagination copies."[47] Smith's version of fellow feeling thus depends on solipsism, but a solipsism necessitated by the fundamental inability of one person to experience what it is to be another. Imagination might be an imperfect tool for understanding the feelings of another, but it is nonetheless the basis for sympathy, and the limitlessness of imagination creates the possibility for rich engagements with the other. Sympathy in the eighteenth century, Marshall describes, is thus "not just feeling or the capacity for feeling but more specifically the capacity to feel the sentiments of someone else," a capacity that "[suggests] the act of entering into the sentiments of another person."[48] Under this schema, "entering into the sentiments of another person" is both possible and edifying. While not refuting the enormity of the influence of Smith and Hume's thinking on the Victorians, I want to suggest that realists ultimately depict the limitations of this kind of fellow feeling. They recuperate the original terms of Smith's construction, terms that emphasized the inability of the senses to "carry us beyond our own perception." They describe scenes and instances where that mirroring does not and cannot suffice because it is predicated on assumption and projection.

Catherine Gallagher's work on Humean sympathy in relation to the eighteenth-century novel is helpful here, as she so clearly renders the paradox of Hume's version of sympathetic extension: ultimately, Hume's sympathy forecloses any increase in knowledge of the other because it is predicated entirely on the self subsuming the other. She asks an important question: "What happens to the otherness of the other people in this process, an otherness already blurred by the relationships described?"[49] It is certainly not retained. Gallagher links Hume's sense of property or ownership—that the closer a person is to the other who deserves sympathy, the easier sympathy is—with the intervention of fiction. Because no one owns the characters in a novel, they are, she suggests, "universally appropriated."[50] Sympathy, Gallagher writes, "is not an emotion about someone else but is rather the process by which someone else's emotion becomes our own,"[51] a construction that models the kind of appropriation Gallagher sees in Hume's articulation of sympathetic extension: to take the sensibility of the other and make it my own. For those followers of Hume (and I mean temporally, not his acolytes), this reading makes good sense. But something shifts in the nineteenth century. This version of sympathetic extension is what the realists attend to amend, I think, by showing within their works that appropriating people, subsuming them into one's self, does not *increase* one's knowledge of the other. Gallagher gestures toward the significance of realist insistence on particularization, in that the more a character is rendered through particularities, the more he or she belongs to the overtly and formally fictional and therefore the more he or she is appropriable and thus fodder for sympathy. In realist works, I wish to say, authors are drawing out the distinction between the reader's (the audience's, in the case of painting) ability to appropriate the represented character and the relationships between people.

As is clear from Gallagher's discussion, separating sympathy from empathy as depicted in nineteenth-century works is made difficult as identification—the feeling "like" associated with the empathy since the word's early-twentieth-century coinage—is aligned so closely with sympathy. Given the influence of Hume and Smith on Victorians and on our understanding of Victorians, it should not surprise that their model of identification-based fellow feeling serves as the most common paradigm for attempts to explain mechanisms of fellow feeling in the nineteenth-century novel. Nor is it surprising that Smith's subtle insistence on insurmountable alterity is overwhelmed by his descriptions of identification from which fellow feeling springs; similarly, the limitations of identification are overwhelmed by its (positive) affective possibilities. Studies of both sympathy and empathy in the novel most often consider the reader as the figure who stands to grow into a state of increased fellow feeling in relation to the characters within. To that end, they consider the readerly identification with characters, as often measurable by the real-world altruistic action provoked by a text. Suzanne Keen's recent *Empathy and the Novel* takes as a given that "character identification often invites empathy, even when the fictional character and reader differ from each other in all sorts of practical and obvious ways," even as Keen notes that complex identification is not required for empathy to arise in a reader.[52] Rachel Ablow develops her arguments on sympathy and the Victorian marriage plot from a similar starting point. While making the distinction between the action- or pity-inducing sympathy she notes in the work of Janice Carlisle and Martha Nussbaum and the fellow-feeling version of sympathy that she describes, Ablow allows that identification is fundamental to both drives and considers sympathy, "as a mode of relating to others and of defining a self," in contrast to those others.[53] In descriptions of both sympathy and empathy, emblematic as they are of the broader critical literature, affective extension or fellow feeling emerges from identification. Despite their prevalence in critical literature, these descriptions do not account for the representations in Victorian literature and painting that depend on alterity. And if these versions of sympathy and empathy guide our engagement with realism, since they both depend on the enmeshing of the other into one's self-conception, aren't we bound to ignore the meticulous representations of alterity on display in nineteenth-century art and literature?

For it is in the depiction of distinctiveness, the sovereign individual, the *different*, that realism excels. In her often-quoted description of the ethical work that novels make possible, George Eliot emphasizes difference as being a necessary prerequisite of the enlargement of affective extension:

> If art does not enlarge men's sympathies, it does nothing morally. I have had heart-cutting experiences that *opinions* are a poor cement between human souls; and the only effect I ardently long to produce by my writings is, that those who read them should be better able to *imagine* and *feel* the pains and joys of those who differ from themselves in everything but the broad fact of being suffering, erring human beings.[54]

At the same time that she's encouraging readers to recognize the traits they share with others—that we are all "suffering, erring human beings"—she also emphasizes that shared experience does not and should not occlude difference. It is easy, when glossing the quotation, to focus on the italicized words "imagine" and "feel." I suggest that we shift our focus to other terms of her statement: Eliot notes that people should be *"better able to imagine and feel"* the other's emotions, and that improvement in ability to imagine and feel is predicated, at least in Eliot's fiction, on first recognizing that you do *not* know the other's emotions.

To be sure, identification is important for the expansion of men's sympathies—what some see as enforced didacticism (in *Middlemarch*, one critic writes, "the moralistic tone of the narratorial voice" scorns and judges the characters within[55]), others regard as nuanced depictions of characters that offer a way for the reader to be exposed to the intimate particularities of another individual, potentially resulting in the self-forgetfulness that leads to sympathy. Felicia Bonaparte makes such a claim about Eliot's works, suggesting they "enlist that completely egotistical bias the reader feels on his own behalf in the forging of sympathy that undermines self egotism." The reader, according to this model, "is surprised into perceiving about others" what he already perceives about himself.[56]

Yet readerly self-forgetfulness or intimate connection with a character does not, cannot explain realist texts and images or—as noted above—the reactions they drew from contemporaries. For these works embrace and depict the limitations of what is knowable. Limits of representation, whether pictorial or textual, collide in the impossibility of representing the interiority of the human other. In *Middlemarch*, Eliot famously describes this choice as a fundamentally practical gesture: "If we had a keen vision and feeling of all ordinary human life," she writes, "it would be like hearing the grass grow and the squirrel's heart beat, and we should die of that roar which lies on the other side of silence. As it is, the quickest of us walk about well wadded with stupidity."[57] In *Le Père Goriot,* that foundational realist text and the same one in which Balzac wrote "All is true," he qualifies the claim by noting that Paris is so vast, a "veritable ocean," that no matter how extensive or comprehensive an attempt to describe it might be, "there will always be a virgin place, an unknown cavern, flowers, pearls, monsters, unknown, wonderful things, forgotten by literary divers."[58] Just as Paris cannot be fully described, so too the other remains perpetually and always irreducible on the page or canvas. In *Le Père Goriot,* longtime residents of the Maison Vauquer can live and eat next to each other for years without having any idea of their neighbors' true emotions, pasts, or even their names.

So the realist must aspire to comprehensiveness while acknowledging that there are real limits to what is knowable, and thus what is representable. Another human individual is the ultimate unknowable. Applying Anderson and Levine's aspirational model of knowledge to affective relationships shows that the attempt-toward is not nullified by the recognition or depiction of ultimate impossibility. In the case of interpersonal relationships, those limits may in fact be seen as constructive: ethics can offer a "configuration of meaning that strikes us as profoundly alien to our wants"; realist characters can capture "an individuality whose very strangeness" inhibits identification.[59] Such perspectives point to a way of understanding the relationships depicted in realist texts and images through analysis of depictions of the alterity of the unknowable other. And because the other is necessarily central in these depictions, and because I wish to emphasize the inassimilability of that other, I will rely on the term "empathy" to describe the affective relationship between the self and that unknowable other.

Empathy and the Other: The Example of Emmanuel Levinas

The relationship with the other is a relationship with a Mystery.
—*Emmanuel Levinas*[60]

Aspirational models of criticism credit a drive toward narratorial (and pictorial) detachment as one of realism's primary achievements. The connection between detachment and the relationships depicted in realist works—relationships predicated on appreciable difference—are those that confound many readers, as they stymie an easy identification. These texts and images tell us that the alterity of the other cannot be overcome, yet their engagement with empathy is undeniable. The argument that an interpersonal ethics can be built on recognition of radical alterity is elucidated with the twentieth-century phenomenological models of Emmanuel Levinas. As I note in the preface, embracing that reading is difficult, in part because we are so conditioned to view alterity as a source of alienation, inhibiting productive interpersonal relationships, and as a block that must be overcome. Levinas's work helps to explain, outside of the frameworks articulated by Smith and Hume, the tendency of realist works to depict failures of communion that arise from one's inability to recognize sovereignty of the individual or inability to escape solipsism. He insists that "the other is alterity,"[61] yet does not place the self and other in a dialectic, suggesting instead that the other remains always unknowable and that out of the unknowability arises ethics and, potentially, empathy. In his account, only another *human* is radically other and cannot be folded into one's self-conception or made into an object of the self. And in his account, the encounter with that radical alterity of the other human opens up the space for ethical behavior. The chapters that follow are not, it must be noted, simply "Levinasian" readings of the works of Dickens, Eliot, Hardy, and Whistler. While Levinas provides a vocabulary to explain the interpersonal dynamics seen in these works, the texts and paintings tell us what Levinas cannot: that the process of recognizing alterity is hard and must be learned, and that the process of learning is akin to acquiring literacy (textual, visual, and otherwise).

Difficulty aside, Levinas does argue that literature can depict the state of the relationship between an individual and the other. Consider his reading of Proust's *À la recherche du temps perdu*, a story that, he argues, develops from an "insatiable curiosity about the alterity of the Other that is both empty and inexhaustible."[62] Proust's development of despair of solitude, Levinas argues, is "an inexhaustible source of hope":

> This is a paradox in a civilization which, in spite of the progress made since the Eleatic philosophy still sees unity as the very apotheosis of being. But Proust's most profound lesson, if poetry can contain lessons, consists in situating reality in a relation with something which for ever remains other, with the Other as absence and mystery, in rediscovering this relation in the very intimacy of the "I," and in inaugurating a dialectic that breaks definitely with Parmenides.[63]

The other must be human because otherwise it could be appropriated by the self (as with objects, commodities, labor, etc.) and it cannot be known by the self—it is the limit case of knowability. If the other were knowable, or understood to be knowable, he or she would merge with the self. As James Mensch frames it, "In reaching the goal, I would not obtain knowledge of the other, but rather self-knowledge. Thus, the other's mental life or consciousness is essentially hidden from me. It manifests an alterity that cannot be overcome."[64] Via this reading, the limit of the epistemological urge intersects with the ideal of detachment: the only true knowledge of the other arises from the recognition that knowledge of the other is an impossibility. Levinas's construction of the unassailable alterity of the other renders impossible the kind of identification on which empathy is built in readings such as Keen's and Bonaparte's. Levinas revives the alterity that Adam Smith describes as being fundamental to human interaction, but where Smith encourages imaginative projection as the (only possible) means to overcome that alterity, Levinas retains the mystery of the other.

The inescapable alterity of the other person is a limit on which ethical action depends. In order to recognize alterity, one must not assume that the other is just like the self, or that oneself is just like the other, but must instead recognize that the gulf between the two is immense, inescapable. That is, before one can empathize, one must apperceive difference. Levinas's descriptions of intersubjectivity are helpful in reconciling the depictions of humans-in-relation presented in artworks with the particular formal and content markers of nineteenth-century realism. Nearly all of the works studied here foreground observation, models of seeing and interpreting, and the variations of visuality include reading and writing.

Before proceeding, I must stop to clarify a point often overlooked when invoking Levinas's philosophy for literary analysis. Levinas's description of alterity and its concomitant ethical demand is a unique aspect of *human* interpersonal experience. Levinasian phenomenology precludes a text functioning as other; anything that can be commodified and appropriated to the self's needs, such as labor or material objects, expressly cannot function as the radically other.[65] The "lesson" Levinas attributes to Proust's novel was contained within it and among its characters and did not result from a reader's relation to the text. Novels, paintings, and other artworks exist firmly within the arena of the material: a book cannot be an other, nor can a painting. And the critical response to Levinas's insistence that the artwork cannot function as other shows how stubborn we readers are in clinging to the belief that viewing the text or painting as other *is* the proper way to engage with art. That stubbornness is evident in the work of literary scholars who, even when explicitly employing Levinas's philosophy as a foundation for criticism, argue that the text can function as the other and therefore as the basis for ethics. David Haney, for example, notes that Levinas does not allow for the relationship between individuals to occur between an individual and a work of art. Nevertheless, Haney advocates this very relationship between reader and text: "one's relation to art can partake of Levinas's own account of the ethical relation to the other."[66] To support this claim,[67] Haney must grant the literary text the overwhelming power of the radically other, and he does: "[the literary text] overflows conceptual structures in a way that gives the conversation the asymmetry one finds in the Levinasian encounter, and thus it is at least structurally ethical."[68] Adam Newton, writing in *Narrative Ethics*, also frames his textual analysis on the idea that "certain kinds of textuality parallel [Levinas's] description of ethical encounter in several obvious ways." Newton suggests that the relationships between the "narrator and listener, author and character, or reader and text" often "precede decision and understanding"; fiction thus "translates the interactive problematic of ethics into literary forms."[69]

I diverge strongly from such approaches, retaining instead the distinct difference between the object (the work of art) and the human other and engaging with the ways that prose fiction and paintings are *not* like persons. I don't mean to deny that readers or viewers engage with texts or images *as if* they did have "lives of their own," to use W. J. T. Mitchell's phrase.[70] And Haney is not unique in demonstrating the propensity to regard an artwork as an other. Social formalism, particularly as defined by Dorothy Hale, depends on a conception of the novel as a unique form that allows readers to access alterity. The novel functions as a way to mitigate the "radical relativism" of pure subjectivity because it can "instantiate both the identity of its author and the identity of the subject the author seeks to represent." By reading a novel, readers can "come to know sympathetically persons who are substantially different from themselves" because the novel functions as that other, "instantiating" both author and subjects.[71] When Hale wonders how much weight to grant "the supposition that the novel as a genre is specially able to represent alterity," it is with the hope of clarifying the longstanding theoretical assumptions that define social formalism. Yet neither she nor Haney recognizes that the very way a novel or a painting can best describe radical alterity is by demonstrating that the formal qualities of art inhibit alterity on all levels. Their readings demonstrate the power of the desire to know the other and to overcome the alterity of the other, and they therefore demonstrate the difficulty that the realist text and image is up against.

My turn to Levinas should not be construed as an unqualified endorsement of his phenomenology, nor can his phenomenology explain the full impact of the realist work (as I discuss below, the artwork tells us something about the recognition of alterity that Levinas's philosophy cannot). Simply put, Levinas's work presents a way to reconcile two seemingly opposing currents in realist works: the insistence on representing the limits of knowledge and the limitation of knowledge embodied in the individual other, and the working toward (the aspiration to) that knowledge. The ultimate end of that aspiration does exist, in a sense, but true knowledge—the hard-learned lesson—is precisely the truism that *one cannot know the other*. These works teach us, as it were, not *how to* overcome the alienation of the radical alterity of the other, but rather that we *cannot* overcome that alterity. It is a lesson, it seems, that we resist as readers and indeed as critics, and if the formulation seems reductive, I can only insist that what may be so simply stated is not nearly—to judge from our reading and critical practices—easily learned. Levinas's staunch devotion to the belief that the artwork cannot function as other articulates a dynamic that these Victorian artists were constructing.

To the degree that these works depict unknowable human characters, the works themselves are emphatically knowable. Further, the very form of these works insists that the artwork is *not* the other. For while analysis of the text might expand the power of a narrative beyond the structures of the novel, each iteration of a novel remains permanently static. It can be held and sold. The same is true for a painting. These finite objects may offer the means to access structures or ideas beyond their boundaries, but they must not be regarded as an other. This is not to say that realist works cannot do the work so often ascribed to them—increasing other-awareness or expanding the extension of sympathy—but rather that their insistence on the unknowability of the other is elemental to that work. *Within* the novels, characters' stories can be learned and manipulated, comprehended and misunderstood, adopted or rejected. While characters may be unknown to other characters within the diegesis of text or image, that relationship is not analogous to the relationship between the reader or viewer and the artwork. The story of a character *is not the same* as the character herself, just as a painting of a subject is not the same as the subject herself. Though novels might represent the wages of alterity between the actors within its covers, or paintings might depict alienation, those are only representations of an encounter with alterity, not the encounter itself. The character within a book may be an other only to other characters within that book, never to the reader. To the reader, those characters are "beings that are shut up, prisoners."[72]

In my analysis of the novels and paintings, this distinction between a human and his/her story is critical, as the works that I examine attest repeatedly that knowledge of another's story does not ensure appreciation of his or her alterity. The failure to make that distinction leads to interpersonal difficulties. According to Levinas's descriptions of interpersonal ethics, the asymmetrical relationship between self and other need not be learned; it simply is. Human existence is already obligated, and that obligation "places the center of gravitation of a being outside of that being."[73] And here is where the Victorian works demonstrate the limitation of Levinas's formulation of interpersonal ethics: as repeatedly demonstrated by the subjects of realist works, apprehending the other (as described in Levinas's phenomenology) seems more often *not* to precede interaction with others. If it is a truth, it nevertheless requires discovery. This process of developing the discernment—and indeed it is a process, born of trial and error, mistakes and missteps—bears much in common with the process of learning.

In light of that process, and in light of the frequency with which these works utilize learning to read as a parallel model for the movement into understanding the other's alterity, I turn to the ideas of "learning" and "literacy" as a way to describe the process of becoming aware of the limits of the self and the resulting awareness. These terms capture the sense of moving-toward that is modeled in the aspirational gestures of the realist works this book considers. The paintings and novels that describe or represent the limits of knowledge through their devotion to accuracy and comprehensiveness parallel the efforts of their viewers or readers, moving into a knowledge whose ultimate goal is the realization of the limits of that knowledge.

I OPENED this introduction with the words of Miss Betsey Trotwood and Turner. Trotwood insisted to her nephew that he did not know what or whom he was seeing, and Turner encouraged his students to adjust their focus so they might learn from what they see. These two moments serve as touchstones for the study that follows: first recognize the limits of your vision, and then learn and work to adjust and improve that vision. The ethical relationship with the other is predicated on the recognition of alterity, though one's focus might preclude that vision, in which case refocusing must take place. One must learn a new means of seeing or understanding. Similarly, shifting focus onto the limits of representation, empathy, and alterity in the novels and paintings that are the focus of this study, texts that have been discussed and analyzed by so many, reveals new ways of understanding them as well.

Given Dickens's extraordinary command of his characters, his remark early in *A Tale of Two Cities* that "every human creature is constituted to be that profound secret and mystery to every other" may seem to be unwarranted. I argue in chapter 1 that Dickens's work demonstrates this truism with a kind of compulsion that belies his preoccupation with the idea, if not its veracity. That every other is a profound secret is not cause for misery, nor does it preclude effective relationships. *A Tale of Two Cities* peels back the layers of awareness within a family unit, showing that those closest to us may be most impenetrable. Dr. Manette's case further reminds readers that one may be a stranger even to himself, while Sydney Carton serves as an example of a most unknowable man who demonstrates the greatest acts of empathy in the novel. *Great Expectations* adds textual literacy as a paradigm for understanding other people. Pip and Joe both learn to read in the course of the novel, but their respective educational journeys serve as contrasts. *Bleak House* wraps identities and relationships in volumes of paper. Documents in Jarndyce versus Jarndyce serve as a wedge to separate people, clouding judgment; Mrs. Jellyby's obsessive letter writing for Africa shows that she has no empathic response to her own family (precisely because they are her own, and not foreign); recognition of handwriting unlocks Lady Dedlock's long-held secrets; and Sir Leicester's three-word message on a slate reveals a man unknown to those who loved him best. Chapter 1 details Charles Dickens's construction of textual literacy as an ability that must be tempered with other versions of literacy: personal, interpersonal, and emotional.

If Dickens's works describe the unknowability of the other, in George Eliot's novels, characters proceed from that opacity toward a position of interdependence or even of recognition, with varying levels of success. The second chapter considers empathy in terms of difference, which allows for a radical reconsideration of some of Eliot's heroines. Hetty Sorrel of *Adam Bede*—consistently labeled a narcissist in opposition to Dinah Morris's altruistic and saintly goodness—is a prime example. Through her late recognition of her inability to "feel anything like" Dinah, Hetty is in fact far more appreciative of the difference of the individual experience than even Dinah Morris. Like Dinah, Dorothea Brooke of *Middlemarch* treads a delicate line between self-abnegation and masochism, so thoroughly imagining herself into others that she fails to define herself as separate. In fact, both failed marriages in *Middlemarch* are the result of one partner's (Lydgate, Dorothea) failure to realize the other (Rosy, Casaubon) as having desires and priorities that are distinct from his or her own. In accordance with her heroines' ambivalent empathy, Eliot insists throughout her oeuvre that empathic extension is not merely ideal but essential to human community, and this chapter reconciles that empathy with Eliot's depictions of both narcissism and altruism.

The third chapter turns to Thomas Hardy's works, which amplify the theme that was only suggested in Dickens's and Eliot's works: that the split between the knowable text and the unknowable person exists not only for the reader of the novel but also within the novel itself. That is, one's identity cannot be conflated with one's story. While personal narratives can be learned, molded, told, and retold, the individual other is and must always be essentially out of reach. Tess Durbeyfield, for example, is separate from the story of her past: the facts of her story may be known, but she cannot be reduced to that narrative alone. Michael Henchard, the Mayor of Casterbridge, cannot distinguish himself from his history once it becomes known, and he cannot trust others to make the distinction; this inability is his tragedy. An explicit consideration of Levinas is crucial to this reading, as his constructions illustrate that we cannot as readers regard the text as embodied or materialized humanity. Because of this, we cannot relate to the text in terms of its difference; there is no face-to-face with a novel, or—as to be seen in the fourth chapter—with an image.

In the fourth chapter, I move from texts to the image plane to focus on the distinction between the object/surface and the subject depicted. The narrative structure common to fiction helps to obfuscate the obstinate alterity of the human other; Victorian narratives insist on teleology, suggest movement toward resolution. Painting, however, does not necessarily suggest movement at all, and Whistler's canvases in particular insist on capturing and perpetuating the tension between subjects. Through aversion and obfuscation in landscape (a trope that connects Whistler's landscapes to Turner's landscapes) and through the use of profile in portraiture, James McNeill Whistler paints images that force viewers to consider the lack of mutuality of their gaze. These methods were used by many realist artists, including Courbet and Manet in France, to create a similar dynamic in their works and for their audience. While not reducing realism to pure convention, these pictorial strategies allow the painter to refuse the viewer *access* without undermining verisimilitude. Through this refusal, Whistler accomplishes a feat parallel to that of the realist authors: he depicts images of people and places that are profoundly moving, yet profoundly unreachable, all the while emphasizing through form the necessity of connection.

As part of their effort to depict life and its processes accurately, realist authors and painters recognize the limitations of their depictions. The author cannot make her characters something other than they are; the painter cannot represent every mystery hidden in his subjects. Rather than being a flaw in the realist doctrine, these limits attest to the realities of life in community with others. That there are others outside of oneself, and that those others exist as the center of their own individual universe, are conclusions earned through experience. Novels and paintings may be utterly knowable, but those they depict—as shown in the works I examine—cannot be completely understood by others within the works. Through their depictions of the appreciation of difference, nineteenth-century British realist works demonstrate that empathic relationships are the result of an awareness of alterity, of the limitations of one's subjectivity and the other's lived experience that rests wholly outside, and not simply the result of identification or similarity. Because empathy may be seated in difference, these works show that it is possible for one to be empathic toward another without being altruistic. This is not a hopeless state, for as the texts examined in *Victorian Lessons in Empathy and Difference* repeatedly show, inscribed in the very movement toward an appreciation of alterity are the seeds of mutuality.

CHAPTER 1

Mysteries of
Dickensian Literacies

By now, most people with even a limited familiarity with Charles Dickens's life are aware of the time he spent as a boy in a blacking factory while the rest of his family was confined in the Marshalsea; as Rosemarie Bodenheimer notes, when it comes to Dickens's biography, "All roads, it seems, lead back to Warren's Blacking."[1] When John Forster's biography of Dickens was first published, however, the details of that long-suppressed episode in Dickens's boyhood were new to most readers, largely because Dickens did not speak about it during his lifetime.[2] Forster presents that period of Dickens's life through an autobiographical fragment that Dickens himself had written, much of which had found its way into *David Copperfield*. Dickens wrote the description of his time spent in the factory from the perspective of a successful author famous for his command of character, yet the fragment is notable for its multiple iterations of uncertainty. Despite his almost painfully accurate memory of the time, and even though he writes about himself, Dickens repeatedly asserts his inability to articulate his own feelings, a tendency attributed variously to repression, to the effects of trauma, or to Dickens's desire to head off doubters:[3] "I am not clear [. . .] it is wonderful to me [. . .] it is wonderful to me [. . .]"; "No words can express the secret agony of my soul as I sunk into this companionship; compared these every-day associates with those of my happier childhood; and felt my early hopes of growing up to be a learned and distinguished man, crushed in my breast"; "That I suffered in secret, and that I suffered exquisitely, no one ever knew but I. How much I suffered, it is, as I have said already, utterly beyond my power to tell."[4]

The final two phrases are repeated nearly verbatim in *David Copperfield*, but similar phrases permeate his oeuvre and are not limited to the quasi-autobiographical. In *Great Expectations*, Pip admits to his "dear Herbert" that "I cannot tell you how dependent and uncertain I feel, and how exposed to hundreds of chances."[5] Such uncertainty is at times due to Pip's inability to assess his own feelings or motivation adequately or accurately: "What purpose I had in view when I was hot on tracing out and proving Estella's parentage, I cannot say" (408). But more common is the feeling of the inadequacy of words to communicate his intended meaning, a meaning often *felt*, and felt keenly and felt specifically: "Words cannot tell what a sense I had, at the same time, of the dreadful mystery that he was to me" (338); "I was so humiliated, hurt, spurned, offended, angry, sorry—I cannot hit upon the right name for the smart—God knows what its name was—that tears started to my eyes" (62); "I tell this lightly, but it was no light thing to me. For, I cannot adequately express what pain it gave me to think that Estella should show any favour to a contemptible, clumsy, sulky booby, so very far below the average" (309). These examples, like those from the autobiographical fragment, are not evidence of a young man who does not know himself, but evidence of a man who knows himself and realizes that to make that self known to another via language is, ultimately, an impossibility.[6]

The prolificacy and scope of Charles Dickens's work often oppugns ideas of limitation. Undercutting critiques of Dickens's proclivity to a totalizing worldview, though not consciously anticipating them, is the regular refrain in Dickens's writing that words are ultimately unable to capture a person, event, place, or feeling. In their very repetition, claims of ineffability become blunted, as the repetition itself is indicative of the effort to overcome the limitations of language. Such insistence on the inability of language to describe feeling or experience is not, I wish to suggest, merely a caveat intended to preclude criticism. Nor is it a supremely personal tic born of Dickens's intense suppression of his own past. This insistence is instead constructive, erecting a foundational boundary that separates people from one another. This limitation inscribes alterity, as it insists that the self must always be a mystery to the other, and the other always a mystery to one's self. Yet that limit is in constant tension with the nearly compulsive drive to overcome it—a necessary urge to connect—that is evidenced through paradigms that offer the potential, or seem to offer the potential, to usurp the boundaries themselves: familial relationships and the communicative exigency of reading and writing. Those paradigms are at work throughout Dickens's oeuvre. Here, I consider the relationships depicted within Dickens's work, outside of their potential influence on the reader's altruistic response. I limit my focus to *A Tale of Two Cities, Great Expectations*, and *Bleak House*, novels in which Dickens inscribes alterity and the limits of the self by insisting on the limitations of reading and the limitations of the familial bond. Always in the presence of those limitations, the often unbearable weight of the impossibility of connection, is an aspiration toward overcoming. These attempts afford the characters and their stories the hope that is reified through the potential of empathy.

The Mystery of A Tale of Two Cities

Early in *A Tale of Two Cities*, the narrator notes a "wonderful fact to reflect upon": that "every human creature is constituted to be that profound secret and mystery to every other."[7] The narrator's fascination is not shared by all of the novel's characters. Many, in fact, seem confident that close friends or family members are perfectly transparent. No mystery, and no secret. The noble Miss Pross, for example, is devoted to her brother Solomon, whose character is permanently and decidedly affixed in her mind and heart. Her gross misjudgment of him is used to comic effect throughout the novel, even long before the terms of their relationship are revealed to the reader. Among its earliest incarnations is her protestation that "There never was, nor will be, but one man worthy of Ladybird and that was my brother Solomon, if he hadn't made a mistake in life" (100). Readers are informed that Solomon was actually "a heartless scoundrel who had stripped her of everything she possessed [. . .] and had abandoned her in her poverty for evermore, with no touch of compunction" (100). Readers may thus reflect on the fact that Solomon is indeed a profound secret and mystery to his sister, but Miss Pross refuses to acknowledge the same.

Miss Pross's comic nature helps to hedge the significance of her idealization of Solomon, though Mr. Lorry does regard her fidelity to her profligate brother as a character flaw. Her loyalty is not, however, merely the optimistic devotion of the family member who chooses to see only the best in any of her kin. It is instead an instance of willed blindness, a commitment to one's own vision of a person, in spite of any evidence to the contrary. She cannot, or does not, recognize Solomon's existence independent of her own vision of him. She cannot grant him separateness, independence from that vision, and in that refusal she confines "him"—which is after all only her understanding of his reality—within her understanding of her reality.

That the closeness of the familial bond can impede rather than facilitate the recognition of alterity is apparent in Miss Pross's relationship with her brother. She is not always so blind to others' true intentions. Her encounter with another other in the novel functions as a useful counterpoint to her interactions with her brother. Thérèse Defarge represents the ultimate threat to those whom Pross holds dear. In the physical struggle that ends in Defarge's death, Pross speaks English and Defarge speaks French; neither is able to understand the other. In this standoff, despite her determined refusal even to attempt to understand Defarge's words, Pross nevertheless discerns the Frenchwoman's intentions accurately, as she intuits Thérèse's desire to kill Lucie. It is, given the circumstances and Mme. Defarge's externalization of her emotion in the scene, not a difficult insight to discern. Robert Alter describes this scene as a "battle between pitiless French savagery and staunch English humanity,"[8] a "symmetric" rendering of polar opposites. That struggle—like the struggle defined by the novel's title—is large in scale, scope, and importance. The entire relationship is predicated if not on a nuanced appreciation of alterity, then on a radicalized notion of opposition. The result is that Pross gets *it* correct while failing to apperceive Solomon's true nature. Though her familiarity with him vastly exceeds her familiarity with Madame Defarge, she cannot see the real character of her brother, proved repeatedly to be a cad. Why the willed blindness? That magical pronoun "my," which should indicate intimacy, instead erects barriers to vision.

Negotiating the spaces between binaries—family versus stranger, mine versus yours—is a task at the heart of the novel. From its opening sequence, the narrative of *A Tale of Two Cities* swings between the best and the worst, heaven and hell. But in addition to the extreme polarities of experience the novel also alternates its focus between the global and the personal, between the expansive vista of London and Revolutionary France and the nearly claustrophobic confines of the Manette household. And to the extent that it is unable to contain the Revolutionary period in its entirety (Dickens's reliance on Carlyle notwithstanding), the novel contrasts the expansiveness of the Revolution with the concentrated intensity of the family unit. The novel's extremes are a suitable setting for the plot points that depend on a lack of discernment on the societal, familial, and interpersonal levels, for the novel is as much about confusion and recognition of identity as it is about revolution. The war was caused by extreme class divisions; Marie Antoinette's "let them eat cake"—reimagined in the novel through Foulon's telling "the famished people that they might eat grass" (231)—is the prototypical example of the wholesale blindness of one person to the plight of an entire people. Utterly unable to imagine the hunger of the poor, her solution is both ignorant (which could be ameliorated with education) and solipsistic (which even education cannot undo)—she collapses the poor and their problems into her own indulged and rarefied existence. A similar dynamic is at work in the novel as it details the difficulty, on the most intimate level, of reconciling the other outside of one's self without collapsing him or them into a mere function of the self.

It thus makes sense that the courtroom drama early in the novel exploits such a blurring between the self and the other—a coup that is repeated at the novel's end, when Carton takes Darnay's place at the guillotine. The two men look alike, but each relates differently to their shared appearance. Carton is effective as a lawyer because of his ability to understand the *inability* of those around him to distinguish between himself and Darnay, a difference that he deeply feels. Surely any novel that depends on mistaken identity or the doppelgänger may make this claim, and there are many. But what distinguishes *A Tale of Two Cities* is its amplification of the polarities of the proximity spectrum: it offers an explication of both the wages of refusing to recognize the other on a global or national scale and the wages of that refusal on a personal scale. The former is accessed through the Revolution, through the French aristocracy's inability to apprehend the poor of their country, for example, while the latter is accessed even through the minor foibles of secondary characters, as in Miss Pross's insistence on her brother's goodness or the luckless lawyer Stryver's inability to recognize that Lucie may not think him a prize husband.

In *A Tale of Two Cities*, the family unit is fraught, serving as the bridge to connect the national or institutional with the personal, and inhibiting the apperception of the other regardless of whether one embraces or rejects kinship. Pross's devotion to her estranged brother inhibits clear vision, but a complete rejection of the familial bond leads to equally problematic results, as demonstrated by Darnay's attempt to distance himself from his familial legacy. In one light, his demission may be read as a recognition of alterity: Darnay chooses to separate himself from his family's deeds and thus his rightful inheritance as heir, marking him as "other." But even within that stance of disavowal, Charles remains unable to understand the implications of this choice for the community left in the countryside of his family seat. His ability to conceive of their experience as it exists independent of his own is feeble. He means well, collecting "but a small installment of taxes, and no rent at all" (242), and he believes he acts on behalf of or for the peasant. Darnay clings to his intention: "he had oppressed no man, he had imprisoned no man; he was so far from having harshly exacted payment of his dues, that he had relinquished them of his own will" (251). Yet his renunciation of wealth is seen by the people of France as an utter abdication—an abdication of his duty to die—and his intention, it turns out, holds no weight in the end.

Darnay does not recognize the impotence or limitations of his view until he sees it defamiliarized, and his first salient encounter with a version of reality outside of his own comes not from those people of France but from Stryver, his ostensible friend. After Darnay admits that he knows the Monseigneur's heir (though not admitting that he *is* that heir), Stryver replies, "I am sorry for it." The reason? Says Stryver, "Here is a fellow, who, infected by the most pestilent and blasphemous code of devilry that ever was known, abandoned his property to the vilest scum of the earth that ever did murder by wholesale" (249). This belief, that Darnay has "abandoned all his worldly goods and position to this butcherly mob," comes as a crushing blow to Darnay, who had thought his actions benign, if not actively beneficent. Yet even Stryver's view is but one of many; it is the view of the British businessman. The French peasantry that calls for Darnay's death among the deaths of all the émi-grés and aristocracy has its own variation on that reality, wherein no repudiation can counter his bloodline.

Familiality can inhibit the recognition of alterity because of the too-closeness of the bond, but also because family ties may be invoked as a means of assigning similarity to a group of individuals. Darnay's predicament evinces the resiliency of the familial bond, as his belief that to renounce that bond is effectively to renounce all its concomitant problems is shown to be erroneous. His situation also demonstrates how brittle ties of loyalty can be. When Darnay functions metonymi-cally as an instance of the cursed Evrémonde race, as he does for Mme. Defarge, his death serves as a means to revenge. Radicalizing the notion of family into race, and including Manette, Lucie, and her children among that race and thus destined for destruction, Mme. Defarge demonstrates the flaw of the mob mentality that marked much Revolutionary violence. It also raises questions of class and the deli-cate balance of recognizing individuality within a regime of wholesale blame. The Defarges' desire for revenge is motivated by a genuine hurt, as her family was brutalized by the Evrémonde family, and so the Evrémonde family (its present incarnation being immaterial) must pay. Those original crimes committed by the Evrémondes—rape, mur-der, false imprisonment—were themselves the product of a regime that reduced entire classes of people to objects. That tactic of *wholesale* alterity (the poor are inhuman, they lack the rights granted by divine intervention to the aristocracy, and thus may be treated as if they were animals) is replicated by the Defarges' revolutionary zeal to eradicate the Evrémonde race (all issue of the Evrémondes are fruit of the evil tree, and therefore deserve death).

Among this landscape of ineffective engagement with difference, *A Tale of Two Cities* does depict examples of a more productive version of alterity, which leads to greater affective connection, if paradoxically through the insistence of alienation. Perhaps it makes sense that within the tangled web of unsatisfying or ineffectual familial bonds, two actors stand emphatically apart through their insistence on difference and refusal of familial bonds. These individuals—Lorry and Carton—share no blood relations with the novel's other characters, yet through and because of their insistent self-alienation and refusal to be considered family are able to create affective bonds stronger than many of those of the novel's blood relations.

Lorry, saddled with the charge of relaying often painful information, twice frames that information in the form of hypotheticals, abstracting himself from the interaction, always unable to reconcile himself and his purpose to the affective charge so often caught up with it. In his earliest meeting with Lucie, when he must tell her that her father is still alive, he cannot articulate his mission. Lucie questions, "'Are you quite a stranger to me, sir?' 'Am I not?' Mr. Lorry opened his hands, and extended them outwards with an argumentative smile" (24). Here, when his body language indicates familiarity with his open, extended hands and smile, his words maintain the ambiguity and estrangement of his position. In these moments of declaration or revelation, Lorry reverts to the conditional or the interrogatory:

> As I was saying; *if* Monsieur Manette had not died; *if* he had suddenly and silently disappeared; *if* he had been spirited away; *if* it had not been difficult to guess to what dreadful place, though no art could trace him; *if* he had an enemy in some compatriot who could exercise a privilege that I in my own time have known the boldest people afraid to speak of in a whisper, across the water there; for instance, the privilege of filling up blank forms for the consignment of any one to the oblivion of a prison for any length of time; *if* his wife had implored the king, the queen, the court, the clergy, for any tidings of him, and all quite in vain;—*then* the history of your father would have been the history of this unfortunate gentleman, the Doctor of Beauvais. (26; emphasis mine)

The repetition of "if" draws attention to the unrelenting nature of Lorry's abstraction. When feelings may prove too intense for Lorry's comfort, he often employs such rhetorical flourishes to create distance or blunt the intensity of emotion. In another typical instance, when Manette has taken to cobbling after his daughter's marriage, Lorry invokes a similar strategy to discuss with Manette the uncomfortable business of his recovery. Wishing to remove himself from the personal interaction, Lorry prefaces the remarks, in which he poses a story of a man in Manette's position to the doctor for his professional opinion, with extensive disclaimers: "I am a mere man of business, and unfit to cope with such intricate and difficult matters. I do not possess the kind of information necessary; I do not possess the kind of intelligence; I want guiding" (208). Only when he has sufficiently distanced himself from the uncomfortable reality at hand is Lorry able to move on to asking the questions that will illuminate Manette's opinions on his own case. Some critics view Lorry's insistence on the distinction between matters of business and matters of the heart as an instance of Dickens's tendency to fragment the conflicting or ambivalent drives of any person into distinct characters; noting Lorry's "fear of emotional involvement, a comfortableness with matters of the head rather than of the heart," Barbara Lecker describes the businessman as a "man whose worldly experience has been solely limited to commercial dealings, and he finds himself disarmed by this new demand on untried capacities."[9]

But a reading that confines Lorry wholly to the world of business overlooks the valuable service of his efforts to abstract himself from "matters of the heart." That abstraction ensures others' comfort as well as his own, as Lorry also anticipates the pain that direct questions might cause; his detachment facilitates his productive anticipation of his friend's anxieties. Lorry's assumption is implied in his framing the interrogation in hypotheticals: Manette is unable to handle direct questioning. Even though this conclusion is not necessarily dictated by the evidence on offer in the text, Lorry insists on it. "Tell me, how does this relapse come about?" he asks, with apparent concern, "Is there danger of another? Could a repetition of it be prevented? How should a repetition of it be treated? How does it come about at all? What can I do for my friend?" (208).

This move toward indirect revelation inserts distance between the members of the familial unit (in which I include Lorry) not only through the form of the interactions but also—and perhaps more evidently—through Lorry's repeated self-descriptions as being "merely" a machine of business.[10] Through this insistence, Lorry manifests an anxiety that is latent for the other characters, for in spite of their shared love, the relationships within the Manette/Darnay family are assailed from all sides: the mother is dead, the father's pain is a mystery that nevertheless determines the family's movements and moods, the husband's background and real name are kept hidden from his wife, the brother is alienated from the sister. Often, characters work to repress or overcome those barriers, with little success. An interesting economy in the novel is that those who are most outside of the family, who insist on their alienation, detachment, and lack of ability to engage affectively, are those who *act* in ways that show extraordinary understanding of the needs and desires of other characters. Lorry is one of these to be sure, and the other is Sydney Carton.

Carton's embracing of his alienation from others, while tiresome for those around him, nevertheless underpins his position as the novel's greatest empathic actor. Like Lorry, he often refuses to admit that he is like others, a caring, feeling person and not a machine. And yet it is in contrast to other characters that Carton's own character becomes most clear, born of his embrace of alterity. Whereas Stryver serves as the foil that exposes Darnay to himself, Carton serves as Stryver's foil. When Stryver acts like a blind idiot when seeking Lucie's hand in marriage, Carton is able to see what Stryver cannot: Lucie would not regard the offer in the same generous light that Stryver does. Carton's uncanny ability to recognize the limitations of others' imagination is predicated on his understanding that you cannot know someone else. Others, Carton knows, imagine that they *do* understand the intentions of those around them. His gift is not exactly that he knows what others think, but rather that he can identify when other people assume to know more than they do. The distinction is subtle; hence it becomes important to distinguish Carton's behavior from others' in the novel. If Darnay's attempts to distance himself from his family are ineffectual, Carton's insistence on utter alterity, the complete distancing of himself from those in his life, may seem overfraught or overdetermined. Yet Carton's behavior leads to the true beneficence that Darnay's actions lacked. In Dickens's telling, the distinction seems to rest on a keener appreciation of difference. It is this skill that renders Carton a "jackal" in the courtroom. He can recognize, and thus capitalize on, the prejudices and predilections of those around him, even if he does not share them. By insisting on the divisions between himself and others, insisting what he is *not* in relation to Lucie's family and his own desire that is bound up with that family, Carton nevertheless manages to eke out an empathic extension that exceeds that of most other characters.

What, then, does the novel endorse, if Darnay's good intentions do not hold up, but the misanthropic, brooding alcoholic becomes heroic because of his profound insistence on *not* joining a family? If recognition of alterity is required before empathic extension can occur, a landscape devoid of appreciation of the sovereignty of the individual would likely indicate a limitation of empathy, especially altruistic empathy. Indeed, the novel and the Revolution itself are peppered with examples—the revolt of the French poor against the aristocracy provides an ideal landscape for the novel's events not only because of the drama inherent in the historical events, but also because the sweeping historical movement depended on a complicated relationship between the needs of entire classes and the needs of the individual. In the French sections of the novel, metonymic or synecdochical substitution of individuals for a class or type of person is treated with particular disdain.[11] Yet those who insist on their difference create a space in which they can act in full consideration or on behalf of the other.

The Lessons of Great Expectations

In *A Tale of Two Cities*, forms of familial bonds frame much of the action of the plot as well as the variations of intersubjectivity depicted. The novel's most heroic actors are explicitly *not* members of the central family. These characters, including Lorry and Carton, work to evacuate the presumptions of knowledge engendered by the familial bond. From the first page of *Great Expectations*, family itself is evacuated of meaning and rendered essentially an invalid construction: mothers are solely mothers "by adoption"[12] and fathers are practically nonexistent. Yet the absence of family ties does not ease the burden of a learned engagement with alterity. One way that *Great Expectations* demonstrates the necessity for such engagement is, in fact, its emphasis on the process of learning. Learning to read serves as one paradigm of broader knowledge acquisition, as it shapes and determines the ways individuals can access the other. When no familial bond originates relationships, they are instead predicated on impression or expectation; forms of understanding that are dependent on the construction of meaning from the apprehension of the external.

Learning to read is bound up with class and social awareness, but having one skill does not guarantee having the other. A disconnect between book learning and its practical application is an early and persistent theme (and a well-documented one[13]), and the novel insists that reading differs from the acquisition of careful discernment. Matthew Pocket, for example, whose home and family are perpetual disasters of disorder, was "a most delightful lecturer on domestic economy, and his treatises on the management of children and servants were considered the very best text-books on those themes" (271). That distinction is lost on Pip, who too easily merges education and class, seeing Joe's illiteracy as "a pity," thinking "when I came into my property and was able to do something for Joe, it would have been much more agreeable if he had been better qualified for a rise in station" (148). Pip's self-centeredness is marked by premature assumptions that he *understands*. Unable to see the imprint of himself upon his readings of everyone else, he fails to recognize their independence from his existence: Pip does not pity Joe's lack of education because of the limitations it means for Joe's life, but rather because it renders Joe less fit for Pip's desire.

Distinctions between education, class, and status are made more difficult for Pip because his inculcation into gentlemanhood seems to coincide with the refinement of his education. Yet while his taste for reading increases, his ability to discern or judge based on that reading does not. Nor is he able to identify his passion within the many possibilities that are now open to him. After he leaves Mr. Pocket's tutelage, he notes, "Notwithstanding my inability to settle to anything,—which I hope arose out of the restless and incomplete tenure on which I held my means,—I had a taste for reading, and read regularly so many hours a day" (312–13). In this way, he is very much like Richard Carstone of *Bleak House*, whose most intense interactions with the law and its paperwork lend him no fuller comprehension of its mechanisms. These readers assign meaning to words on a page—reading in its most literal sense—but do not derive meaning from the pages in their entirety; they read lines, but cannot read between them.

Variegations in scrutability and education are continually bound up in the plot, making clear to the reader the difficulty of extricating one from the other. For example, upon arriving in London, Magwitch greets Pip with expectations of a performance of gentlemanly attributes, and foremost among them is the role of books in the apartment and in Pip's life. Pip's "fine and beautiful" linen and his dandy-making clothes are trumped by his books. Magwitch enthuses over the number of volumes Pip owns, "mounting up, on their shelves, by the hundreds," but also over their difficulty and inaccessibility, signs that the convict reads as indicators of class. Comprehension is immaterial: "You shall read 'em to me, dear boy! And if they're in foreign languages wot I don't understand, I shall be just as proud as if I did" (320). But Magwitch's relationship with reading cannot be reduced only to a signifier of social status, and in describing his own education, it becomes clear that reading functions for him as more than a sign of class; it is also an indicator of humanity, allowing for the building of connections between people:

> Tramping, begging, thieving, working sometimes when I could, [. . .] a bit of a poacher, a bit of a laborer, a bit of a wagoner, a bit of a hay-maker, a bit of a hawker, a bit of most things that don't pay and lead to trouble, I got to be a man. A deserting soldier in a Traveller's Rest, what lay hid up to the chin under a lot of taturs, learnt me to read; and a travelling Giant what signed his name at a penny a time learnt me to write. (347)[14]

Learning to read and write appear at the end of Magwitch's narrative of his evolution, following a variety of odd jobs—a bit of this, a bit of that. This adaptability, learning trades enough to scrape by, is set in opposition to Pip's scholarly pursuits, which render him essentially inflexible and filled with knowledge that has little practical application. Textual literacy becomes, for Pip, instead of a means to understanding, an impediment to the multiple kinds of reading he must learn to do. He must learn to adapt his book learning to situations where it might better enlighten or enrich his comprehension of events and people outside of books.

Before he learns that lesson in adaptation effectively (and whether he does by the novel's end is debatable), Pip's ability to interpret nontextual signs and actions is notoriously limited. Miscommunications arise comically when Mrs. Joe is confined to her bed after she has been attacked. Without speech, she must make her desires known through a slate and Pip must interpret her intended meaning from her murky signifiers: "The administration of mutton instead of medicine, the substitution of Tea for Joe, and the baker for bacon, were among the mildest of my own mistakes" (122).[15] These particular substitutions lead to mild mistakes indeed; but substitution also figures in Pip's *greatest* mistakes, which arise from substituting himself in place of the other.

Interpretation, or rather misinterpretation, delivers its most devastating consequences in Pip's continual misreading of those around him, Estella in particular. Pip regularly assesses a person or situation and draws incorrect conclusions: he believes Miss Havisham to be his benefactor despite repeated reminders from Jaggers that the facts do not bear out the conclusion, and he is convinced Biddy (who, as an excellent, "self-forgetful" reader, is the first to interpret accurately Mrs. Joe's slate-written symbols) is "grudging" and "envious" of his good fortune. Both mistakes have grave consequences; as is true throughout the writing of Dickens as well as Eliot and Hardy, misreading people is most debilitating when it results from a refusal to accord the other alterity.

Pip seems to know that his interpretation of people depends on his relationship with them; when Estella protests that Pip will forget her soon enough, he rejoins: "Out of my thoughts! You are a part of my existence, part of myself. You have been in every line I have ever read, since I first came here, the rough, common boy whose poor heart you wounded even then" (364). Yet he cannot allow that the influence of his adoration of Estella has a real effect on his ability to discern meaning from the signs—or direct statements—she offers. This is most clear in Estella's continual assertions that she is not what Pip believes her to be, and his refusal to take in that fact: "'You must know,' said Estella, condescending to me as a brilliant and beautiful woman might, 'that I have no heart—if that has anything to do with my memory,' I got through some jargon to the effect that I took the liberty of doubting that. That I knew better. That there could be no such beauty without it" (237). Pip insists that he knows Estella better than she knows herself. The terseness of the last two sentences indicates the narrator's distance. The older Pip, from a better-informed and reformed position, can see the folly of those conclusions, but in Pip's youth, his schooling did little to counter his predilection to believe in his idealized Estella rather than the living, empirically existent woman who spoke to him. Despite her protestations, Pip can only stubbornly insist on his incorrect reading of her: "When should I awaken the heart within her, that was mute and sleeping now?" (244). Here, Peter Brooks notes, Pip "is claiming natural authority for what is in fact conventional, arbitrary, and dependent on interpretation."[16] And Pip's interpretation depends to its detriment on his desire. When Pip says, near the novel's end, that his life's been a "blind and a thankless one," the blindness has been on display throughout the narrative: he refused to see what was in front of his eyes all along.

It is worth a moment to detour from Pip's centrality to consider how another character may be understood if one considers the recognition of the alterity of the other as a central motivation of empathic extension. Estella's insight, which Pip characterizes as condescension, can in that light be read as a compassionate attempt to grant Pip independence from her desire. Pip routinely mistakes Estella's feelings or meaning, but Estella is able to assess Pip's thoughts and motivations accurately, often attempting a corrective intervention. She does so on more than one occasion (e.g., when Pip chides her for flirting with Drummle and not him, she asks him with a "fixed and serious" expression, "Do you want me, then, to deceive and entrap you?" [311]). What can account for this insight? One might argue that she demonstrates a Smithean imagination about Pip, understanding his desire by imagining what she might want in his position. But if Estella demonstrates the mechanism of sympathy that Smith described, she also revives the predicate to sympathy that Smith described: she is more acutely aware of one's ultimate inability to know "what other men feel."[17] Estella was raised to function as a proxy for Havisham's thwarted desires, and her survival depended on her ability to carve out alterity under those circumstances, to individuate herself as a unique person even as she was aware that to do so explicitly would draw censure. Pip, on the other hand, was forced to feel as an other throughout his youth, and sought to overcome any innate sense of alterity rather than to engage it. Though she maintains a self-conscious distance about Miss Havisham's intentions for herself, Estella appreciates (through that very detachment) that Pip has willingly accepted the role Miss Havisham designed for him. In this way, Estella—much like Biddy—understands that Pip's feelings for her are different from hers for him. Pip, unable to replicate that movement, dismisses Estella's comments too easily, reducing them to the work of the coquette, rather than realizing that Estella is anticipating or attempting to mitigate Pip's desire (a fact that is not undermined even if the cruelty of her comments indicates her own desire).

When Pip asserts that Estella had been in every line he'd ever read, it would have been more accurate to say that *his desire* had been in every line; *he* had been in every line. That tendency extends to his interactions with other characters, and is on particular display in two instances when Pip sees himself defamiliarized. In both scenes, Pip reacts with horror to the speech acts or revelations of the two father figures: Joe and Magwitch. But just as Pip (Philip Pirrup) is a version of his birth father (Philip Pirrup), he is also a version of each of these two fathers. Some read his responses to Joe as the shame of Joe's persistent lowness and inability to adapt or change or learn, thus putting the onus on Joe's innate inability.[18] In fact, Pip's response is more likely a transference of his own shame, as can be seen when Miss Havisham makes Pip the gift of money to bind his apprenticeship. In this moment, Pip has been in her company for some time and has become accustomed to her peculiarities and to the peculiarities of Satis House. Through this interaction with Miss Havisham and with Estella, he has altered his notions of propriety, politeness, and station, and concurrently developed a sense of shame about himself, a sense he lacked prior to his introduction to Satis House. When Joe meets Miss Havisham, it is near the end of Pip's engagement with the residents of Satis House. Pip, now familiar with Havisham's ways, is mortified by Joe's behavior toward the woman, behavior that is undoubtedly motivated by the shock of weirdness to which Pip is now accustomed. During this encounter, Pip is in a position to witness a repetition of his own first performance from the perspective of his relative enlightenment. His horror and shame arise, then, equally from recognizing the mistakes and awkwardness of his own first encounter at Satis House through more knowing eyes. Joe's mistakes were Pip's mistakes; Pip's new viewpoint was then Miss Havisham's and Estella's. Pip's horror is thus a form of self-recognition, and suggests more about his self-conception than about Joe's poor breeding or ill manners. If Pip hates Joe for his embarrassing behavior, it is a transference of self-hatred.

The same relationship occurs during the scene when Magwitch reveals that he is Pip's benefactor. Magwitch has sought to make Pip a gentleman through money he has given Pip anonymously; Pip is horrified at the prospect that a low man believes he can, through the gift of money alone, buy status. Pip is shattered because his illusions of being intended for Estella are shattered, but that discovery would lead to disappointment, not disgust and revulsion. His visceral response to Magwitch is more likely the result of Pip's recognition of his own folly. He can now see, from his vantage of greater experience and exteriorized from the position of belief, how faulty Magwitch's proposition is, how flawed the idea that any money, earned any way, may purchase station or class. But recognizing that fact in light of Magwitch's presence illuminates the more piercing, personal truth: that Pip anxiously, readily, and joyfully accepted that same proposition. To then recognize that Magwitch made the same assumption implicates Pip in Magwitch's image—not because of any obligation to the convict, and not because of any of Magwitch's actions—but because Pip wanted to believe it to be true as much as Magwitch did. Again, Pip's recoil is the recoil at his own folly, as reflected in Magwitch.

Pip thus accords a repulsive alterity to those who repulse him and refuses it to those who seduce him. Learning to overcome that tendency leads Pip to more productive relationships, with himself and with others. Through the trope of literacy, *Great Expectations* explicates the role of the individual in recognizing alterity: it is a syntax that can be learned, but such learning requires a pupil willing to extricate himself from the textbook.

The Invisibility of Text in Bleak House

Apprehension and appreciation of the other are made difficult by the familial bond, as shown in *A Tale of Two Cities*. Even in the absence of family ties, achieving fluency in such recognition is not easily gained, as shown in *Great Expectations*. Similar distillations are more difficult in *Bleak House*. It was written before *A Tale of Two Cities* and *Great Expectations*, and in it the terms of encounters with alterity are not so easily defined by blood or by faculty. In this "document about the interpretation of documents,"[19] reading, writing, parentage, language, and fidelity are inextricable.[20] The role of writing is unquestionably important in the novel, so much so that many suggest that Dickens's point in *Bleak House* is to represent the distinction between the hard, mechanical world of the law and the potential of individual feeling to ameliorate the harm caused by the law. David Cowles argues that Dickens privileges "deeper human truths" as opposed to the world of facts defined by Chancery; these "inner, human truths," Cowles argues, "make a character—and presumably the reader—a better person, that is, more sensitive to others' needs, more loving."[21] If there is indeed a deeper human truth advocated by the novel, it is—I argue—tied inextricably to the harm arising from the refusal to acknowledge alterity. This limitation is meted out by the novel's very structure, where Esther, though central to her own narrative and the *fabula*, is never mentioned in the third-person narrative. She is "absent from half the book,"[22] to put it one way—the third-person narration seems not to know Esther at all. If Lady Dedlock's fate offers a stark cautionary tale, it is because her character reveals what may be lost (what *is* lost to her, lacking the interference of a Carton or the time to grow allowed to Pip) when an individual is unable to grant a thorough separateness of feeling and experience to those around her. This fate, her fate, is bounded both by words and by her kindred.[23]

As was the case in *A Tale of Two Cities*, *Bleak House*'s minor characters function as reductions of the more difficult and complex relationships at work elsewhere in the novel.[24] Mrs. Jellyby famously serves as one such figure, her telescopic philanthropy showing her willingness to embrace the very different other, the African distanced physically and culturally from her. Her own children's desperate need of attention, affection, and care, however, goes unheeded. Mrs. Jellyby's usual state is to be "very busy," her "whole time" taken up with the African project: "It involves me in correspondence with public bodies and with private individuals anxious for the welfare of their species all over the country. I am happy to say it is advancing."[25] It is easy to see Jellyby's characterization as an indictment of such philanthropic endeavors and the self-satisfaction they inspire, due in large part to the protection against exposure to true pain, poverty, and hunger afforded by distance. But in terms of the novel, the critique of the effects of their mother's devotion to her cause on Caddy, Peepy, and the other Jellybys is a much heartier indictment than the critique of the abstract notion of telescopic philanthropy itself, or the imperialism that encourages it. A mother who can "see nothing nearer than Africa" (52) is sadly inattentive toward her own children and blind to the results of that neglect.[26] Caddy is regularly covered in the ink of her mother's enterprise, and must eke out an existence outside of that charity work; and she does, eschewing education or the educated in favor of a dance teacher whose father's pretensions to aristocracy are as absurd as Mrs. Jellyby's pretensions to humanitarianism. Mrs. Jellyby can accommodate the radical difference of the masses of African poor rather than the individual other in her own family. As in *A Tale of Two Cities*, where the French aristocracy exhibited a willed blindness to the poor within their own country, Mrs. Jellyby embraces the plight of the *very* different while the needs of those in her own backyard, so to speak, are unnoticed and unmet. Bruce Robbins, in his analysis of Jellyby's "telescopic philanthropy," suggests that Esther's version of philanthropy is the novel's imperfect alternative to Jellyby's distanced efforts; by accepting a face-to-face engagement with Jo, Robbins notes, Esther "literally loses her face" to smallpox.[27] In his reading, the enforced distance (what might also be called detachment) of Jarndyce or even Skimpole is thus, in some ways, preferable to the direct intervention of Esther.

Proximity is not the only variable for such concern. I am interested more in the individual's conception of intersubjectivity than with conceptions of social responsibility or philanthropy engendered by perceptions of closeness and duty. Jellyby's relationship to her African project is interesting because it illuminates her alienation from her own family: she is simultaneously too close to them and too detached from them. Lady Dedlock is consumed with one much closer to home, and her inability to conceive of her husband outside of her overdetermined self-conception leads to results that are even more disastrous than the plights of the Jellyby children. Like Michael Henchard in Hardy's *Casterbridge*, Lady Dedlock has so defined herself by her own history that she cannot imagine that others would respond to it differently than she does. To be sure, her self-definition is built upon a denial of her past, but the sheer affective charge of that denial ensures that the past is ever part of the present. That it is a site of misery and shame is, for her, an unalterable truth. This truth speaks to Lady Dedlock's acceptance of shame as a part of her self-conception, but also as a readable, indisputable existent.

Equally indisputable is the misery that this shame ultimately causes her. The novel suggests that her death was unnecessary; her husband forgave her and her daughter sought her, outcomes that were inconceivable to her. Lady Dedlock's internalized shame and the intense effort she musters to repress it seem to arise from a devotion to the propriety so prized by her husband and her own devotion to the image of dispassionate cultivation that others associate with her character. Curiously, it also results in a meager, ungenerous view of those she loves, as she imagines that they would choose not to forgive her sins, should they be discovered. It is a view that demonstrates her entrapment in her own interiority. She cannot conceive that Sir Leicester, a man who loves her, would be able to forgive her what she cannot forgive herself. She cannot imagine his conception of her being anything other than her self-conception.

Lady Dedlock's actions are determined by her anticipation of what others will think, the narrative voice adopting her own anticipation: "her shame will be published—may be spreading while she thinks about it" (854). She is not wrong in her expectation. When her past becomes known, the gossipmongers do consume the news from her estate: she is, in town, "for several hours the topic of the age, the feature of the century" (886). Dickens blunts the power of the intense focus by ironically emphasizing its brevity, showing that even major tempests blow over quickly. So while Lady Dedlock anticipates the intensity of the response, she cannot imagine that her shame, like all "features of the century," will quickly blow over in the minds of others; in her mind, that shame has been hers eternally ("the thunderbolt so long foreseen by her" [854]), and she conceives of her public condemnation as having the same power and same duration as her private condemnation. In this moment, she too lacks the words to communicate her own fear and dread: "The horror that is upon her, is unutterable" (854). This Dickensian insistence on the ineffability of a feeling, that which cannot be communicated and thus cannot be understood, is shown to be the real horror of her situation: the problem is not that the horror itself is so strong, but that in feeling that it cannot be communicated, that no one could understand that horror and thus calm it or neutralize it. The speaker ceases to believe that communication is possible, that amelioration is possible, and that human connection is possible. And in this moment human connection is most desperately needed.[28] To feel the impossibility of communication without making an effort to reach outside of herself, however futile, Lady Dedlock excludes all possibilities of response to her, and condemns herself: "There is no escape but in death. Hunted, she flies" (855).

Lady Dedlock's flight demonstrates the hopelessness that defines her comprehension of her situation (which is not at all the same as her situation itself). As her life was built upon controlling the information others had about her, she is unable to recognize that the revelation of her unknown past could lead to any reaction other than the one she most fears: she cannot imagine that alterity can itself be predicate to a positive, enriching interpersonal engagement. This tangle is problematic throughout *Bleak House,* not only for the characters but also for readers who expect resolution through unification or integration. Carolyn Dever notes that the scene when Esther is holding her dead mother "should be the most profoundly integrated moment of the novel," but is instead "among the most disturbing" because of Esther's discomfort with being at once an "agent of forgiveness" but also at the mercy of the will of her dead mother.[29] Why should this be a moment of integration? Esther is discovering her mother, but also discovering that she is *not* her mother, a realization that might be painful but is ultimately necessary for Esther's movement into selfhood. The exclamation that Dever cites, "it frightened me to see her at *my* feet," articulates Esther's sense of ambivalence: in the moment of discovering a connection she so longed for, Esther must also be surprised by the impossibility of that connection.

A great tragedy of *Bleak House* is that through Lady Dedlock's attempts to control entirely the knowledge that others had about her-self—a stance that depends on the belief that she can know entirely what others know—she renders moments of growth and affection impossible. Though some of Lady Dedlock's anxiety about the reaction to the revelation of her past was founded, for her husband, to whom she mattered most, her past mattered least, an outcome Lady Dedlock could never have imagined. Sir Leicester also recognizes what others think about his wife, but notes that response only in order to register his dissention from those points of view. Characterizing her departure as a mere "misunderstanding" that "deprives" him of his "Lady's society," Leicester insists to those in witness that her standing in the household and in his heart stands unabated. His speech on the topic, all the more lucid for its following a period of shock-induced muteness, is—as the narrator notes—"honourable, manly, and true":

I am on unaltered terms with Lady Dedlock. That I assert no cause whatever of complaint against her. That I have ever had the strongest affection for her, and that I retain it undiminished[. . .] My lady is too high in position, too handsome, too accomplished, too superior in most respects to the best of those by whom she is surrounded, not to have her enemies and traducers, I dare say. Let it be known to them, as I make it known to you, that being of sound mind, memory, and understanding, I revoke no disposition I have made in her favour. I abridge nothing I have ever bestowed upon her. I am on unaltered terms with her and I recall—having the full power to do it if I were so disposed, as you see—no act I have done for her advantage and happiness. (895)

His speech is gallant in its elegance, but it is not the first example of Leicester's attitude toward his wife after he has learned of her past. The first iteration of his response, while still inhibited by the fit that felled him, was a mere three words, written on a slate for Inspector Bucket to see: "Full forgiveness. Find—" (858–59). Here Sir Leicester, of all people, exhibits an ability to know precisely what Lady Dedlock's fear will be: that she will be shamed and judged and that he will feel the thunderbolt "so unforeseen by him" (854) such that it will destroy his ability to love her. He immediately and correctly identifies this reaction and moves to forestall it, both in Lady Dedlock herself and in those around him who may expect otherwise from him.[30]

"It is wonderful to me"

Before concluding, I will take a moment to turn to one of Dickens's works most associated with the production of active sympathy—and most associated with the potential for texts to encourage altruistic action resulting from readerly sympathy—his "Christmas Carol."

Audrey Jaffe, following Adam Smith, conceives of Dickens's sympathetic project in terms of the instantiation of spectacle. Describing "A Christmas Carol," she notes, "As a model of socialization through spectatorship, the narrative posits the visual as a means towards recapturing one's lost or alienated self—and becoming one's best self," a process thoroughly grounded in the reader's identification with the text: "That identification accounts for the story's apparently limitless capacity for transformation."[31] Jaffe acknowledges that the transformative power of the story is connected to its ability to commodify its themes and its characters; she writes that the story "constitutes itself as an endlessly sympathetic commodity, its variable surface reflecting an unchanging reality to embody readers' and spectators' desires."[32]

If the power of the "Carol" is in the spectacle of the misery of the Cratchits, then that complete and easy commodification is what makes

"A Christmas Carol" more of a fairy tale and less of a realist text. The turning of person into spectacle, an act that fundamentally denies the human-ness of that person, is perhaps the last sympathetic act possible. To the extent that such spectacle encourages empathy, it's a cheapened version, one predicated on the extension of one's own desire or concern, and ameliorating it (as Scrooge does, as readers might) simply means shutting up the representation, turning the human other (and not the text or its theme) into an object of the self. But something more also happens within the "Carol," and certainly within Dickens's longer fiction. Paul Saint-Amour offers a compelling reinterpretation of the affective power of the "Carol," writing that the real moral crux of the tale occurs through Scrooge's unwillingness and inability to look upon what might be his own corpse. The encounter awakening Scrooge's sensibilities is not the consumable spectacle of the Cratchits as being his equal, his fellow travelers in life, but rather the encounter with the instantiation of himself outside of himself: the self defamiliarized, made other.[33] It is a spectacle that Scrooge refuses, in doing so recognizing that as death is one unknowable instantiation of the self, so too is the human other. Via his refusal to remove the veil covering the corpse, Saint-Amour writes, Scrooge says, "Let me not pretend to domesticate my death; Let the future remain both unforeclosed and undisclosed, its face hidden; Let me recognize others, for all that they may be untranslatably alien, and for all that I may owe them a responsibility without limit, as 'fellow-passengers to the grave.'"[34] It is this engagement, this realization of the things that cannot be commodified and which must remain insistently beyond identification, that defines Scrooge's movement into action.

In the works considered in this chapter, which are representative of Dickens's oeuvre, a pattern emerges. The heroic actors surprise. The "wonder" that marked Dickens's descriptions of his own life when it was most incomprehensible to him is revived in these characters, whose actions seem similarly inexplicable, and in many ways, wonderful. Carton, Lorry, Estella, Sir Leicester, Scrooge: those described by themselves or by the novels as worthless, mere machines, narcissistic, and proud, are nevertheless able to appreciate the fundamental and ultimate difference of the other, an appreciation that allows for action. It is often imperfect action, not always altruistic (the young Estella is a good example, knowing via their face-to-face encounter precisely how to most pain the young Pip), but their movements toward empathic extension suggest that their insistence on alterity is necessary to facilitate movement outside of oneself. These characters' encounters with the limits of themselves are reflected in Dickens's writing: the compulsive insistence on ineffability from a hand capable of producing voluminous words; the closest bonds of family shown to inhibit connection; the terms of reading shown to inhibit understanding; the master character-maker admitting that every man is a mystery to every other. Through such admissions and bindings, these texts replicate the working toward recognition that defines the struggles toward connection described within.

CHAPTER 2

Sawing Hard Stones

Reading Others in George Eliot's Fiction[1]

"Book Second" of *Adam Bede* (1859) begins and ends with depictions of reading and writing. Its final chapter, "The Night-School and the School-master," details both the promise and the difficulty that the people of Hayslope face in their quest for education. In church, they do not hold prayer books because "not one of them could read,"[2] but there is a palpable desire among the common workers to learn despite very basic challenges. Bartle Massey's schoolhouse offers them the opportunity, in the evening and after long days of physically exhausting work. Learning to read is no less exhausting. Bill, a young stone-sawyer, "found a reading lesson in words of one syllable a harder matter to deal with than the hardest stone he had ever had to saw," because he was unable to discern differences between letters, noting that they are so "'uncommon alike, there was no tellin' 'em one from another'" (253). But Bill, and others like him, continues to try, and the narrator identifies this slow process of becoming literate as a humanizing act: "It was," the narrator remarks, "almost as if three rough animals were making humble efforts to learn how they might become human" (255). In the chapter that opens "Book Second," "In Which the Story Pauses a Little," the authorial voice famously interrupts the story to justify her creation, commanding that artists not exclude from their works the "common, coarse people" who populate the world. For art to portray that world more completely, artists must change their subject choices, and readers and viewers must alter their expectations. In this extranarrative disquisition, Eliot implores readers to be patient and charitable, to expand their understanding of art, and, by doing so, to expand their sympathies: "the way in which I have come to the conclusion that human nature is loveable," she writes, "has been by living a great deal among people more or less common-place and vulgar" (201).

The link between Eliot's entreaty and Bartle Massey's work in the schoolroom may seem obvious: in Eliot's vision, readers of *Adam Bede* are like Massey's pupils, who, through their efforts to read, are working to expand their own humanity. *Adam Bede* exposes readers to the "com-monplace and vulgar," and the exposure will expand their sympathies and make them more tolerant of their fellow men. That simple parallel may comfort some readers (who think that they are being edified merely by reading a novel) and frustrate critics (who protest Eliot's pedagogical or pedantic overtones). But surely such a conclusion is *too* simple, for it overlooks what Eliot so strongly emphasizes throughout *Adam Bede*: learning is a difficult, mostly slow, and often painful process, made all the more difficult by instances in which readers are lulled into believing that meaning is self-evident. All versions of discernment, it seems, entail a learning curve. Even "nature's syntax,"[3] which ought to precede any academic refinement, can be grossly misleading if read too hastily or without careful deliberation. Just ask Adam Bede. Adam's misinterpreta-tion of Hetty Sorrel's beauty is costly, but he is not the only poor reader of "nature's syntax" in Eliot's oeuvre.

Perhaps more so than any of the other writers addressed in this study, Eliot describes literature's potential to expand her readers' largesse with-in her prose, and the mechanisms for that growth into other-awareness are mirrored in the repetitions of narrative dynamics throughout her works. Focusing on *Adam Bede* and *Middlemarch*, this chapter addresses Eliot's approach to representing intersubjectivity, an approach typified in these novels (one early and one late) but one that is evident throughout her works. I am concerned with interpersonal relationships depicted *within* her novels and via their form, as opposed to readerly engagement with empathic extension. This focus distinguishes my readings from those of others who address the ways that Eliot engages her reader in the empathic or sympathetic process, including those by Rachel Ablow, Ellen Argyros, and Suzanne Keen. Certainly Eliot was concerned with the effect her novels might have on their audience, but if the edification is to occur through exposure, then surely it is important to understand how empathic process is depicted within the novels.

Unlike Dickens's depictions of other-awareness, Eliot's works empha-size the process of becoming. Whereas Dickens's characters often either are or are not other-aware, a distinction that seems to depend on an individual's intrinsic nature, Eliot's depictions build on Dickens's by rendering this awareness as the result of a process. Eliot confirms not only that the encounter with the radically different other is a startling, sometimes painful process, but also that it is not a static encounter. For Eliot, engaging in the development of other-awareness offers the potential for growth; connection through language becomes possible only after the self recognizes the other as ultimately unknowable. To be sure, Eliot's plots are determined by the ability of characters to navigate their own identities, but they are also determined by their ability to navigate alterity. Eliot's oeuvre is populated by unfulfilled lovers, ignored family members, misunderstood and misunderstanding protagonists, each of whom undergoes a version of Adam's struggle to recognize Hetty independent of his idealized vision of her. Essential to interpersonal literacy is learning one's limits and understanding the limits of learning.

The recognition of difference instantiates one such limit. As is the case in *Adam Bede*, Eliot's statements about the goals of art often stress the potential for expanding fellow feeling. These moments are undoubtedly well-trodden ground for the critic, but it is worth revisiting some—if only briefly—to note that the emphasis might fall somewhere other than those places that garner most attention. Eliot's letter to Charles Bray in which she argues that art must "enlarge men's sympathies," for example, is remarkable for her insistence that the expansion occurs toward those who are not *like* oneself but instead *differ* from oneself, "in everything but the broad fact of being suffering, erring human beings."[4] The distinction is important. Too often in art, comfortable idealizations intrude upon the actual, impeding the recognition of alterity rather than facilitating it. Such idealizations are built upon the familiar and the non-threatening; they propose that what is known or desired is broadly representative of what *is*. What must also be embraced is the possibility of the unknown. A lack of knowledge may be mitigated by learning based on what is apart-from-the-self, but for that to happen one must move beyond easy identifications or assumptions. J. Hillis Miller astutely notes that in Eliot's works, those easy identifications or assumptions are often predicated on thinking of the other via analogy of the self, what Miller calls "figurative displacements," along with the inherently solipsist position of the self as the center of everything and everyone surrounding.[5]

Eliot's most consistent means of representing the movement outside of identification into a perception of difference rest on describing the limitations of what is known or what is knowable; assume you know too much and risk misunderstanding or shutting down the possibility of genuine empathic response. Consider the opening of "The Natural History of German Life." Eliot contrasts an individual having limited knowledge of the railways with someone who has an intimate familiarity;

their relative knowledge determines the richness of "the range of images" called up by the mention of the word "railways." When human beings are the focus of concern, both individually and collectively, the stakes are much higher, and the epistemological certainty that one might have about the railways, for instance, is disrupted. Yet the easy dependence on idealized versions of fellow man is tantalizing for artists and their audience precisely because it provides a sense of certainty—regardless of how unwarranted—and both groups embrace artistically influenced and often euphemistic ideals of the rural poor or other groups of people with whom they lack intimate familiarity.[6] Understanding or interpreting others is made more complicated when one cannot even see them clearly; art may thus cloud interpretation, rendering viewers less literate, less aware of the other's lived experience:

> Only a total absence of acquaintance and sympathy with our peasantry, would give a moment's popularity to such a picture as "Cross Purposes" where we have a peasant girl who looks as if she knew L. E. L.'s poems by heart [. . .]. The notion that peasants are joyous, that the typical moment to represent a man in a smock-frock is when he is cracking a joke and showing a row of sound teeth, that cottage matrons are usually buxom, and village children necessarily rosy and merry, are prejudices difficult to dislodge from the artistic mind, which looks for its subjects in literature instead of life.[7]

That such poems or paintings (Eliot also takes to task Holman Hunt's *The Hireling Shepherd*) were popular supports Eliot's point that audiences prefer the trouble-free version of country life perpetuated by art. Here and throughout "German Life," Eliot also emphasizes the difficulty of an artist rendering an image free of idealized virtue of the rural poor, given how engrained in the collective imagination and artistic convention those idealizations are; "falsehood is so easy, truth so difficult," as she writes in *Adam Bede*. But the difficulty in rendering images that work against idealized notions of the other *is* a fact of reality and, in addition to bemoaning it, Eliot works to include such myopic vision in her characters. For example, *Middlemarch's* young, idealistic Dorothea Brooke, who seeks out suffering where others seek to avoid it, is disappointed when the curate of her new husband's estate describes his peasants in terms similar to those of "Cross Purposes":

> Everybody, he assured her, was well off in Lowick, not a cottager in those double cottages at a low rent but kept a pig, and the strips of

garden at the back were well tended. The small boys wore excellent corduroy, the girls went out as tidy servants, or did a little straw-plaiting at home: no looms here, no Dissent; and though the public disposition was rather towards laying by money than towards spirituality, there was not much vice.[8]

On the one hand, the passage is critical of the curate, who is unable or unwilling to describe the cottagers outside of an artificial veil of contentment. On the other hand, Dorothea does not question his assessment. While Dorothea is concerned with the welfare of others, she still imagines others' suffering in terms of herself; though she feels "ashamed," she regrets there is not more suffering at Lowick, so that she would have a greater function there.[9] Dorothea lacks curiosity beyond her interests, and both characters fail to reconcile these Lowick strangers with their own predilections or desires. These failures do not indicate a hopelessly flawed character; instead they demonstrate the thorough difficulty of accurately understanding the other, perceiving his position, reading his intentions.

Eliot's writings, from *Scenes of Clerical Life* through *Daniel Deronda*, regularly depict such fissures in identification or recognition. Eliot often details the impediments to interpersonal understanding through the inclusion of extreme reactions to alterity: solipsism, wherein one cannot regard the other independently of one's needs or desires, and self-abnegation, wherein one desires to sacrifice the self entirely to the other. Although these positions seem to sit at opposite ends of the spectrum of human interactions, both refuse to grant the other independence or autonomy. Navigating the gulf between the two extremes requires a tempering of self-regard in relation to that beyond the self—much like the tempering of metal, this requires an encounter with a force that might, in other circumstances, be debilitating. Such efforts are not always successful, and the aspirants are not always the heroines of the novels, but Eliot's invocation of *learning* as the means to achieve the desired end validates efforts toward that tempered recognition and underscores the idea that appreciating alterity is a process and not an inherent quality.

Learning Not to Feel: Hetty Sorrel as Moralist

Since the publication of *Adam Bede*, reductive readings of the characters of both Dinah Morris and Hetty Sorrel have persisted: Methodist preacher Dinah is good, saintly, and selfless, while dairy maid Hetty is flawed, deviant, and selfish. In her 1883 analysis of Eliot's works, Mathilde Blind invoked this formulation, describing Dinah as "a beautiful soul; whose spring of love is so abundant that it overflows the narrow limits of private affection, and blesses multitudes of toiling, suffering men and women with its wealth of pity, hope, and sympathy" and Hetty as a "shallow, frivolous little soul" who hides a "hard little heart" under her "soft dimpling beauty."[10] Over one hundred years later, Judith Mitchell echoes this characterization, noting again that Hetty's "shallow, selfish nature"[11] opposes Dinah's benevolence. Mitchell further suggests that Dinah's heroism is due not only to her selflessness but also to her beauty acting as a "true signifier" for her good soul, whereas Hetty's exterior beauty is a "false one."[12] By continually placing Dinah and Hetty in such formulations—good/bad; selfless/selfish; true signifier/false signifier—much of the past scholarship on the novel only supports these bifurcated categories, when in fact the novel seeks to break up these easy formulations.[13]

Adam Bede's rural setting is a particularly apt environment in which to document the necessity of nuanced "readings" of people because judgments are admittedly made based solely on appearance. This community and the assessments its members make offer a version of judgments that readers are likely to make, and when the characters' assumptions are proven incorrect, the critique applies to the metanarrative as well. Mrs. Irwine, who insists that nature would not make "a ferret in the shape of a mastiff," is a typical voice within Hayslope. She declares: "[no one can ever] persuade me that I can't tell what men are by their outsides" (72). Not mere entitlement or snobbery, this attitude cuts across class lines; Mrs. Poyser frames a similar comment in terms she knows better, saying, "Some cheeses are made o' skimmed milk and some o' new milk, and it's no matter what you call 'em, you may tell which is which by the look and the smell" (104). Mrs. Irwine and Mrs. Poyser, as the novel shows, are wrong. Nature may encode the body with messages about the soul, but they are neither explicit nor easily interpretable.[14]

Common critiques that Hetty is simply a soulless ego (her "vanity and selfishness," one critic argued, lead not only to her own "terrible crime and shame," but to "misery for others!"[15]) overlook what is achieved by reducing others' apprehension of her to pure surface: Hetty becomes a kind of text to be interpreted, allowing the novel to function as a critique of the ways her exterior is read. Hetty is above all a hard text to read, and the difficulty of reading her is emphasized precisely because she *seems* to be such an easy text to read. Committed to enhancing her attractiveness, Hetty furthers the readable distance between her interior and exterior.[16] She presents—via her body, her expressions, and her actions—an obstacle to easy legibility, as her startling beauty leads others to form more generous opinions of her than actions support. Serving as an obstacle, forcing those around her to challenge their own interpretive skills in this way, Hetty performs a valuable function for the community she otherwise defies. Further, she is shown to be able to recognize, finally, the limitations of her own interpretative powers. In these ways, Hetty does far more work in the novel than playing the role of a hard-hearted beauty; Hetty may just be the best teacher the novel has to offer.

The relationship between Hetty's beauty and its message for others is linked to Hetty's lack of interiority, her simplicity of mind, and her inability to care for others in situations that normally generate a caring response. Her limitations in this regard are often read as an indication of her narcissism. After Thias Bede's funeral, for example, Hetty meditates not on the family's loss but on her many suitors and her power over them. Eliot asks the reader, "In this state of mind, how could Hetty give any feeling to Adam's troubles, or think much about poor old Thias being drowned?" (111). How could she indeed. Hetty is *aware* of others—aware of their presence insofar as it acknowledges her own presence. But to imagine them as being analogous to herself,[17] to imagine their interiority, is beyond her powers because of her youth, her self-centeredness, and the cocoon of leniency granted her as a consequence of her disarming looks: "Young souls, in such pleasant delirium as hers, are as unsympathetic as butterflies sipping nectar; they are isolated from all appeals by a barrier of dreams—by invisible looks and impalpable arms" (111). Her youth and capriciousness are important considerations if one is to appreciate Hetty's humanity and understand the limitations of empathy. Here, as in other novels, Eliot is determined that "the reader understand all the extenuating circumstances pleading for" her characters, a way to explain—if not excuse—their behaviors.[18] Coming into awareness is, Eliot insists, a process.

Complicating a reciprocal understanding between herself and her community is Hetty's refusal to engage fully in the agreed-upon community order, a resistance seen as petulance and not individuation. She fails to recognize alterity because she fails to recognize those around her at all, one might say, except to the extent that they reflect her self-conception. Although aware that others judge her exterior, Hetty at first does little to internalize that knowledge or apply it to her interactions with them. This egoism is literalized through her inability to read texts. The narrator notes that she "had never read a novel: if she had ever seen one, I think the words would have been too hard for her" (148). Her ignorance of novelistic romance left Hetty without a frame in which to place her own experience, without "a shape for her expectations" (148). It also meant she lacked exposure to representations of another's interior experience, the very possibility ostensibly presented by novels (such as *Adam Bede*) for their readers. Her limitations in reading underlie broader difficulties in communicating and in living within a community. She is, for example, chronically late, either misreading clocks or unable to reconcile clocks set at different times. When scolded for arriving home late, she responds, "I did set out before eight, aunt [. . .] but this clock's so much before the clock at the Chase, there's no telling what time it'll be when I get here" (158–59).[19] Failing to negotiate the real difference between her family's time and "gentlefolk's time," Hetty is out of step with her household. Given her difficulty differentiating between the trappings of the life she has and those of the life she wants, it is not surprising that she has difficulty deciphering handwriting. When she attempts to read the letter in which Arthur breaks off their relationship and dashes her hopes at marriage, instead of devouring it she can only read it slowly, despite the fact that "Arthur had taken pains to write plainly" (361). The gentleman's "handwriting" is meant both figuratively and literally. Arthur believes (as he tells Adam) that he had been explicit about his intentions with Hetty—but not only can she not read his writing, she cannot discern his true intentions.

The faults of Hetty's character—her egotism and inability to become part of a community—argue for the flatness and simplicity of her persona. Yet while Hetty is a poor reader of novels and letters, she is felicitously aware that others constantly read her. It is this gift of insight that lifts her from being a purely one-dimensional character. Her studied primping displays a vanity that is both controlling and controlled, through which she can affect the conclusions others draw about her. It is an extraordinary command; she constructs her visage and demeanor in such a way to ensure that her affair and her pregnancy are not discovered. She is vain, to be sure, but early in the novel she merely seeks confirmation that her vanity is based on beauty perceivable to others. Once her circumstances change, she seeks confirmation that the changes in her body are *not* perceivable to others, and this requires considerable manipulation on her part. While readers are told that, "on Hetty's blooming health, it would take a great deal of such mental suffering as hers to leave any deep impress" (366), Hetty becomes aware of the necessity of controlling her countenance so that her pain cannot be read. Rather than *accentuating* her charms, she must now *enact* charm to disguise her pain. She demonstrates a kind of active self-control that is new in her character, catalyzed by the shattering of her illusions: "She must not cry in the day-time: nobody should find out how miserable she was, nobody should know she was disappointed about anything; and the thought that the eyes of her aunt and uncle would be upon her, gave her the self-command which often accompanies a great dread" (366). At this point, she finds the self-command that is not told on her face, and her interiority changes though her exterior does not. By maintaining a veneer of her old self, Hetty is able to manipulate the readings of many in her family and community, and those who never read past her surface are sufficiently convinced by her (purely) superficial composure. By anticipating those reactions, Hetty demonstrates an ability to recognize how others perceive her—how she appears from the outside.

More importantly, Hetty's active construction depends on the complicity or inattention of those around her, since they must be poor readers to overlook the tale her body eventually tells against her will. The novel reminds its audience that reading is a two-way street; in Hayslope, Hetty can write her body but the community has to join in the reading. Hetty's work to manipulate others' readings of herself is thus, for the most part, effective. Only the astute Adam recognizes a change in her, noting that "there was something different in her eyes, in the expression of her face, in all her movements [. . .]—something harder, older, less child like" (383). While his love-induced blindness causes him to cast his observations in a most generous light, believing the best about his bride-to-be, not all of her community has such a compelling excuse to support their overlooking the obvious. Perhaps the greatest misreading of all is that no one in Hayslope notices Hetty's pregnancy—the *most* visible, physical sign of Hetty's past actions and present anguish as well as a visible sign of the social upheaval caused by a landowner breaking rank to prey upon a dairy maid. It cannot be understood, however, that Hetty was simply adept at hiding her pregnancy, because when she leaves Hayslope to find Arthur, her "condition" is immediately detected: "the stranger's eye detects what the familiar unsuspecting eye leaves unnoticed" (408). Surrounded by the unchanging context of Hayslope, changes that defy expectation or defy the community's existing understanding of Hetty are not read by her family or friends, and Hetty's pregnancy is not seen.

Hetty's relationship with her community is then one of mutual, perhaps even willed, misunderstanding. It is easy to place the blame completely on Hetty. In his introduction to the novel, for example, Stephen

Gill concludes that Hetty's "tragedy" is that she has neither a "lively sense of others" nor "a feeling for [her] place in the present and past community."[20] Barbara Hardy argues that Hetty's self-absorption and lack of sympathy in response to the death of Adam's father demonstrate her rejection and neglect of the community. Hardy further suggests that "to be a deviant from the community is to be in serious danger, and ultimately to endanger and disturb the entire community."[21] Hetty does deviate from the community, and the consequences of her actions are soon clearly wrought upon her and those she loves. Her disgrace and her isolation are, however, not solely her fault. When confronted with the true weight of her actions—leaving—her illegitimate child to die—residents of Hayslope recognize the damage wrought by their failure at educating Hetty or educating themselves about her.

Of course, readers are privileged to information that Hetty hides from those around her. Readers know that beneath the dimpled exterior lies a narcissistic liar; the information readers can access serves as a corrective to the misinformation Hetty's controlled face and manners present to those around her. Those critics of Hetty who insist she is the true inverse of Dinah are lulled by this impression that the novel provokes. Yet Eliot employs in her novel's structure many of the same techniques that Hetty used to her own advantage, and to the same end. The novel demonstrates that its audience, like those in Hetty's community, may be poor readers too: *Adam Bede* coaxes readers into thinking that we understand this girl, just as those in Hayslope think they understand her. Hayslopians think she's a sweet dear thing; readers of the novel think she's rotten to the core, but both conclusions are incomplete. Eliot's plot insists that Hetty can fool her community, that impressions-based assumptions of knowledge are dubious at best: those in Hayslope think they can *see* her and that therefore they know her, and novel readers also believe they can read her accurately. But surely the novel insists that our satisfaction in understanding Hetty is, like her community's, unwarranted. The novel encourages in readers the same self-smug belief that Adam and Dinah share, establishing a level of comfortable certitude, which is then challenged.[22]

Eventually, Hetty's community learns what readers have known (her affair with Arthur; her narcissism), and if we may judge by the voice of critics, both object to her egotism and to her crime. Because loveliness is celebrated, because it is naturalized as good, Hetty's moral grounding is expected to be equal to her physical beauty. Falling short of that overreaching expectation, Hetty is denounced harshly by much of her community and by many readers.

But while those around her may be grossly disappointed in her, Hetty shows herself to be cannily aware of her own limitations. When in jail and Dinah tries to convince her to repent, Hetty responds, "I can't feel anything like you" (489). This line is not evidence of Hetty's selfishness; it is instead a crucial moment that establishes Hetty's awareness of Dinah's alterity. Hetty's self-centeredness makes her weirdly better able to maintain the gulf between herself and the other. This moment is essential because Hetty grasps that others remain unknown and unknowable to her. Though the admission is in one sense condemning, it also shows that Hetty understands herself in relation to those around her.

Hetty is able, in this most fraught moment, to realize something that even the pious Dinah cannot: Hetty acknowledges the fundamental differences between her reality and the expectations of her community. In this encounter, Dinah tries through the only means she knows to bring Hetty to confess, an evangelical argument, replete with promises of release from pain and promises of eternal comfort after death. In her sermon on the green, which introduces Dinah to Hayslope and to the novel, she seized upon Chad's Bess's vanity, threatening Bess with damnation should she fail to repent and calling Bess a "poor blind child" (36). Now, in Hetty's cell, Dinah calls upon the same strategies, framing Hetty as a blind child whom Dinah must lead to the Lord and his forgiveness. Hetty—let's not forget—is imprisoned for the murder of her child, whom she bore to a man she loved and a man she thought loved her, after her hopeless journey seeking that man. Dinah, who consistently seeks pain and suffering and seems, in fact, to derive a kind of pleasure from it, speaks to Hetty as if she is personally aware of the devastation Hetty feels: Dinah asks Hetty, "But isn't the suffering less hard when you have somebody with you, that feels for you—that you can speak to, and say what's in your heart? . . . " The ellipsis seems to indicate that Hetty is silent, and Dinah waits. Then it is Dinah who answers her own question: "Yes, Hetty" (488). What eventually sways Hetty to confess is the same fear that sways Chad's Bess. It is not a movement into love, but a giving in to the fear that Dinah has cultivated—a fear of the unknown that she promises to ease through her religious certainty. What Hetty *does* say indicates her awareness that Dinah's engagement with the spiritual realm is beyond her comprehension: "I can't know anything about it"; "I can't feel anything like you" (488–89). When has Dinah admitted that her knowledge of the other—others' needs, others' feelings, others' priorities—is limited? She cannot even acknowledge that she does not fully know herself.[23]

The moment recalls another in "The Two Bed-Chambers" chapter, wherein Hetty and Dinah are contrasted: the one self-centered, gazing into her mirror, and the other focused on everyone but herself, looking out her window. In that moment, Dinah rushes to Hetty, seeking to offer her services as confidante or confessor, pleading with Hetty until she finally begins to cry. Lest the reader regard this scene as one of good, selflessness triumphing over cold-hearted egotism, the narrator intervenes:

> It is our habit to say that while the lower nature can never understand the higher, the higher nature commands a complete view of the lower. But I think the higher nature has to learn this comprehension, as we learn the art of vision, by a good deal of hard experience, often with bruises and gashes incurred in taking things up by the wrong end, and fancying our space wider than it is. (175)

Later, when in jail, Dinah reminds Hetty of her offer of friendship that night at the Hall Farm. Then, instead of the narrator providing the corrective, it is up to Hetty to do what she can to call Dinah into the realization that she has not yet learned to comprehend Hetty. Hetty's corrective to Dinah's imploring—"I can't feel anything like you"—is a corrective to the reader as well. For the reader in this moment, Hetty insists on the insurmountable difference between herself and Dinah, and in her simplicity and even her selfishness, she gives way to an awareness of difference that Dinah works so hard to elide. The reader can in this moment see what Dinah cannot: Hetty's insistence on alterity, that the human other must never be foreclosed, is one of the novel's great lessons; the novel presents through its omniscient narration the ability to see what is at that time unknown to Dinah. Dinah, at the end, moves into a more nuanced understanding of herself, which requires her opening up a space for what she had thought impossible—that she could marry someone she loved. She must allow herself to be surprised, a movement that comes in the novel after her encounter with Hetty and (moreover) her colliding with her own desire that was itself a surprise, and not always a welcome surprise.

Learning Not to Help: Dorothea as Masochist

Like Dinah, Dorothea Brooke of *Middlemarch* (1871–72) treads a delicate line between self-abnegation and masochism, so thoroughly imagining herself into others that she fails to realize a distinct separation between herself and them. Her marriage to Casaubon is the central example of this dynamic. She bases her actions and choices in response to Casaubon on an idea of him; unfortunately, that idea/ideal is itself based upon her misinterpretations of his desires.[24] In fact, both failed marriages in *Middlemarch* are the result of one partner's (Lydgate's, Dorothea's) failure to realize the other (Rosamond, Casaubon) as having desires and priorities that are distinct from his or her own. If these are models of empathic extension, the results are hardly encouraging. Through its multiplotted structure, *Middlemarch* features multiple characters engaged in relationship dynamics that are not unlike those in *Adam Bede*. Whereas my analysis of *Adam Bede* focused on Hetty as a misread individual, in *Middlemarch* I first turn my attention to she who misreads: Dorothea. As in *Adam Bede*, in *Middlemarch* the novel's very form encourages the apperception of limitations. An omniscient narration lends a feeling of comprehensive understanding to the text. It is a feeling Dorothea shares: she believes in her ability to cut through communal fallacies to the truth of a situation or idea, she believes that she has access to a higher purpose and understanding hidden from others. That belief, as we will see, is tempered. And just as Dorothea is surprised, other characters surprise as well. A Casaubon, a Rosamond Vincy may seem to be eminently knowable to other residents of Middlemarch, but as Dorothea comes to learn, those easy conclusions are often shown to be false, and if not false, at least based on a projection of the self.

Dorothea's evolution from a self-sacrificing helpmate, both unsatisfied and unsatisfying, to something else has long attracted attention of those who attempt to situate her behavior with regard to Eliot's intended instruction.[25] Eliot's famous metaphor of the pier glass offers a basis for one interpretation, extolling the reader to remember that every individual is the center of her own universe, and that around her center all others serve merely as constellations. Characters in the novel exhibit such awareness with varying degrees of success. The novel too works toward this end, forcing the reader to switch perspectives, as when it poses that self-reflexive question "Why always Dorothea?" (278).

Yet Dorothea is interesting because she seems from the novel's opening to insist on her alterity, to insist that she is unlike all others. The novel supports Dorothea's fundamental difference from those around her by pairing her actions or responses with those of another character: her reaction to Sir James with Celia's reaction, her ambitions to Lydgate's ambitions, and her relationship with Ladislaw versus Rosamond's. In part, she becomes complacent in her perceived radical alterity and thus cannot negotiate herself among the others around her, and this complacency poses an obstacle to richly mutual relationships with her friends, family, and neighbors. By grouping all of those people into a massive "other" and asserting herself in opposition to them, Dorothea nurses a self-righteousness that is destructive. She, like the omniscient narrator, affects knowledge of all. Dorothea is committed to working against the conventional, and although the young woman might believe that she accords independence to others as to herself, the novel demonstrates that she has instead constructed the collective other purely out of her self. Their ostensible alterity is instead an inversion of Dorothea's dearly held opinions and beliefs.

To Dorothea, her sister Celia seems to be a representative of conventionality. But Celia actually exhibits a corrective moderation to Dorothea's earnestness. Even Celia's nickname for her sister, "Dodo," indicates the contrast between the sisters: to Celia, Dorothea seems both as antiquated as the extinct bird and as foolish as the word has come to imply.[26] Celia sees plainly what Dorothea often refuses to acknowledge, and she informs Dorothea of this difference, telling her sister that "You always see what nobody else sees; it is impossible to satisfy you; yet you never see what is quite plain" (36). Celia relishes the moments when she can prick the soap bubble of Dorothea's mind: "She dared not confess it to her sister in any direct statement, for that would be laying herself open to a demonstration that she was somehow or other at war with all goodness. But on safe opportunities, she had an indirect mode of making her negative wisdom tell upon Dorothea, and calling her down from her rhapsodic mood by reminding her that people were staring, not listening" (32). A further reminder of the disconnect between what people actually thought of Dorothea and what she imagined they thought is communicated in Celia's understanding that to contradict Dorothea would be to declare "war with all goodness."

The distinction between staring and listening is a subtle one to recognize or understand, and here Celia demonstrates an awareness and command of life in society with others that Dorothea cannot. It recalls the relationship between Hetty and Dinah. Though regarded as the less serious of the two, Hetty has a more sensible grasp of the community than Dinah does. And Dorothea, like Dinah, exists on aspirations that ennoble her and set her apart from that community. But that imposed separation ultimately inhibits the connection she so longs for. Dinah wants to touch others through religion, and Dorothea through good works, but neither can effect her desired result in part because of their overdetermined, insistent self-differentiation. Theirs are not genuine encounters with radical alterity, but rather inverted projections of the self onto the wholesale "other."

Dorothea is only one of many perpetrators of this version of self-centered-ness. Her uncle reads Dorothea in light of his own critique of her ideology: she is too religious, and thus when "She was an image of sorrow," her uncle "at once concluded Dorothea's tears to have their origin in her excessive religiousness" (37) without curiosity about their true origin. And the good Sir James also misreads Dorothea, interpreting her reactions according to *his* own predilections and preference: "Her roused temper made her colour deeply, as she returned his greeting with some haughtiness. Sir James interpreted the heightened colour in the way most gratifying to himself, and thought he never saw Miss Brooke looking so handsome" (30). So Dorothea is not wrong to object to such characterizations, which are to her indicative of communal views in general, though she regards herself as immune to such solipsism.

And thus Dorothea works diligently to set herself apart from the vague plural others, and in some cases her contrariness is simply that. When Dorothea is in Rome on her honeymoon, Will Ladislaw is astonished by her unwillingness to enjoy or even appreciate the city's rich artistic offerings. And when she comments on his own artwork, finding it uninspiring, she offers as a consolation: "I never could see any beauty in the pictures which my uncle told me all judges thought very fine" (206). Whom does she deprecate with this statement? Any humility about her inability to appreciate art is undercut by the implicit critique of her uncle and, by extension, "all judges." Hers is truly a remonstrance against all who are not her, or all who do not share her unique perspective. At this point in the novel she is only beginning to recognize that her husband, the one man whom she has given her approval (and her submission), differs from her imagined version of him. It takes considerably longer for her realization to spread to others: if she had misunderstood Casaubon, might she have similarly misjudged "all judges" whose ideas she had rejected?

Is Dorothea thus the only one out of balance in an otherwise sane world? Is the mob necessarily correct? The narrative voice seems to indicate not: in some cases, Dorothea's peculiarity seems as such only in relation to others, and others, the narrator reminds, might actually be the odd ones after all: "She would perhaps be hardly characterized enough if it were omitted that she wore her brown hair flatly braided and coiled behind [. . .] at a time when public feeling required the meagerness of nature to be dissimulated by tall barricades of frizzed curls and bows, never surpassed by any great race except the Feejeean" (27). Yet even in this seeming defense of Dorothea, who rails against the unnatural fashions of her day, the narrator struggles to articulate the description:

the phrasing "would perhaps be hardly characterized enough if it were omitted that" is remarkable for its murkiness.

If Dorothea represents the complexities of adapting self-abnegation to a relationship with others, *Middlemarch's* Rosamond Vincy offers an alternate model of the complications facing the individual-in-community. Rosamond Vincy shares with Hetty Sorrel distractingly good looks, family and friends who indulge her whims, a solipsistic worldview, and—in the end—a moment in which she escapes, perhaps surprisingly and fleetingly, from that solipsism. Both women are also mischaracterized by others, who often believe that a pliant and sweet exterior indicates a similar disposition. The novel's development of Rosy's relationship with Lydgate provides a basis for development that Hetty lacked: their interaction offers the reader examples of mutual oversight and misunderstanding nearly equal in their depth and frequency. Such misunderstandings are not, the novel emphasizes, due to a lack of concern or due to neglect: "Between him and her indeed there was that total missing of each other's mental track, which is too evidently possible even between persons who are continually thinking of each other" (587). Thinking *of* the other does not ensure thinking *as* the other or thinking *like* the other. Their problem is not simply one of missed mental tracks, an image that suggests each recognizes that the other has a separate mental track and might look for it only to miss it—overlook it, jump it, and so forth. Instead, both Lydgate and Rosamond are bound to their own mental tracks, and each has configured the other in terms of him- or herself—they lack an appreciation of genuine, or radical, alterity.

Lydgate's vision of Rosamond and his expectations of her as a wife are so self-centered and self-indulgent that the narrator marks them as fantasy; his early vision of her existed in a "dreamland" wherein she "appeared to be that perfect piece of womanhood who would reverence her husband's mind after the fashion of an accomplished mermaid, using her comb and looking-glass and singing her song for the relaxation of his adored wisdom alone" (583). Even before their marriage, then, Rosy functioned for Lydgate as an example of an imagined perfection, and his vision required a wife to revere and adore her husband exclusively. She was a type, an ideal, and a type of mermaid, not even human.

Tertius Lydgate is not alone in this vision, as Rosy's unrealistic expectations and imagination matched his before their marriage and received an equally harsh blow from reality: "The Lydgate with whom she had been in love had been a group of airy conditions for her, most of which had disappeared, while their place had been taken by everyday details which must be lived through slowly from hour to hour" (661). So each partner indulged in nearsighted fantasies about the other, and they built a marriage upon unuttered expectations that were, from the start, impossible to fulfill. Throughout the novel, though, Rosamond's view of Lydgate is shown to be no momentary lapse in an otherwise thoughtful, rational, expansive mind, but rather a natural by-product of a soul who valued her own circumstances to the exclusion of all others:

> In fact there was but one person in Rosamond's world whom she did not regard as blameworthy, and that was the graceful creature with blond plaits and with little hands crossed before her, who had never expressed herself unbecomingly, and had always acted for the best—the best naturally being what she best liked. (665)

Rosamond's eventual turn outside of herself is thus both unexpected and hard-earned. She was not used to recognizing the desire, or even the existence, of the other, "except as a material cut into shape by her own wishes" (777), and so the encounter with a person and experience profoundly different from her own is a painful process, described in one instance as the other's feeling being "burnt and bitten into her consciousness" (779).

The coming together of Rosamond and Dorothea stages a meeting of those two kinds of self-centeredness in Eliot's fiction—one who sacrifices herself at all costs and the other who promotes herself at all costs, and achieving an accurate mutual understanding is both complex and shocking:

> It was a newer crisis in Rosamond's experience than even Dorothea could imagine: she was under the first great shock that had shattered her dream-world in which she had been easily confident of herself and critical of others; and this strange unexpected manifestation of feeling in a woman whom she had approached with a shrinking aversion and dread, as one who must necessarily have a jealous hatred toward her, made her soul totter all the more with a sense that she had been walking in an unknown world which had just broken in upon her. (796)

It is the harsh reality that intrudes violently upon Rosamond's consciousness. She experiences a "great shock," her "dream-world" is "shattered," and the realization "breaks" upon her. One source of this intense intrusion of an alternate reality into Rosy's mind is the realization that her previous assumption about Dorothea's character was false. The alternate understanding of Dorothea that "shatters" Rosy's previous opinion, described as it is in negative and even violent terms, is a *less* antagonistic, more positive view of Dorothea. That is, Rosy recognizes that Dorothea does *not*, in fact, "necessarily have a jealous hatred towards her." While that information may be comforting, while it may render Dorothea more friendly or approachable in Rosamond's eyes and perhaps allow for the generous turn of Rosamond's actions, the realization of her alterity is not easy for Rosamond because it requires freeing Dorothea from the long-held internal definition Rosamond maintained.

Negotiating the self in relation to the other, whether an individual or a collective, depends on accepting the limitations of the self rather than acknowledging empirical reality, a distinction that is mirrored in the shape of the realist novel. Seen in this light, the scene in which Mrs. Cadwallader encourages Dorothea to "exert" herself "a little to keep sane, and call things by the same names as other people call them by" (537) appears to be less about the pressures of the bland majority of Middlemarch forcing Dorothea into a state of conformity than it is about Dorothea's difficulty reconciling her version of reality to those versions experienced by others. Her "stout" response to Mrs. Cadwallader, "I never called everything by the same name that all the people about me did" (537), demonstrates her persistent clinging to her personal vision even if it leaves her woefully out of step with others. Theirs is a conversation about language, about the naming of objects. If we believe that language serves as the basis of the ethical relationship,[27] to refuse to communicate is to shut down the possibility of ethical communion—curiously, something flatly at odds with Dorothea's stated desires. Further, Middlemarch's parochial social scene is genuinely chafing to Dorothea's temperament. Middlemarch is described early in the novel as a place where "sane people did what their neighbors did, so that if any lunatics were at large, one might know how to avoid them" (9). And yet Dorothea's uncle, who is undeniably a game neighbor, and who ensures his sanity according to the status quo, nevertheless implores Dorothea to reconsider her marriage plans, which he views as conforming too rigidly to her set expectations: "But there are oddities in things," he argues, "Life isn't cast in a mould—not cut out by rule and line, and that sort of thing" (41). She struggles "in the bands of a narrow teaching, hemmed in by a social life which seemed nothing but a labyrinth of petty courses, a walled-in maze of paths that led no wither" (29). But Dorothea works through that struggle, learning her way through the maze; Eliot's realism depends upon her depiction of that negotiation, that process of learning the stakes of living in relation.

Altruism and the Affect of Learning

Recognizing that not everyone operates in the same manner as oneself is—as depicted in Eliot's fiction—a difficult, though learnable, proposition. Despite the difficulty of that recognition, and despite the very real possibility that one may never reach perfect insight, working toward this realization is imperative and contains the promise of the kind of empathic extension the author endorses. It is through this working-toward that humanity proves itself. The impossibility of reaching the ultimate realization is no deterrent. Such aspiration resonates with the realist goal: to describe accurately and comprehensively the human condition may be an impossibility, but as a goal the desire elicits no bad faith.

In Eliot's fiction, that impossibility is rendered through tropes of illegibility and illiteracy. Those who read others often draw mistaken conclusions; those who are read are often read incorrectly. A shared unwillingness to recognize this possibility of misreading or being misread demonstrates why characters such as Hetty are such a problem—it is not because they are inherently bad, but because they are too easily misread. They present cases where others' assumptions are wrong; they embody the realist doctrine of unknowability. Within their plots, both Hetty and Rosamond are sacrificed—Hetty to death in America, and Rosamond to a life of banality—but both present the obstacle that another must encounter on the way to growth, serving as a check on easy assumptions. Such characters instantiate the knowledge that the insurmountable difference between individuals is not due to beauty, ignorance, or any other particular physical or personal trait. The unknowability of the other is instead inherent and universal. Eliot's narrative voice is complicit in this lesson, as its tone is one of certainty, and the narrator affects an accurate omniscient comprehensiveness that individuals must necessarily lack.

With her focus on learning, Eliot forestalls the ease of immediate access, a point supported through her portrayal of both extremes: the narcissist whose beauty (for example) leads to her being misread, and the self-abnegating characters, whose inborn or ingrained desire to help others still requires a movement into genuine awareness of alterity before their good intentions can be fulfilled. That awareness must not be a function of insisting that oneself is different from everyone else—the kind of wholesale alterity that marks Dorothea and Dinah. They are confusing to their communities. They are misunderstood. Unfortunately, both women insist upon this difference as a matter of point, and yet in doing so end up denying the kind of unique sovereignty to those who make up their community as well as to themselves.[28] Even the seemingly most understanding, most compassionate person must learn.

The importance of that *process* is made evident in Eliot's *The Lifted Veil*,[29] whose main character, Latimer, has the ability to experience others' consciousness, and with that ability he ought to be perfectly suited to life within Eliot's universe. There seems to be no greater human facility within Eliot's oeuvre; as Sally Shuttleworth puts it, "Latimer is granted the gifts George Eliot deemed crucial to narrative art: an ability to enter into the minds of others, and the power to foresee the future."[30] Latimer's "previsions" or "presentiments" do not, however, ensure productive affective relationships, but rather the opposite. His is a miserable and lonely life, and his only sustained interest in another human being was directed at a woman who presented "the only exception" to Latimer's "unhappy gift of insight." About his future wife, Bertha, and Bertha alone, he was "always in a state of uncertainty." Such uncertainty is tantalizing, even if only to the extent that it allows Latimer to maintain his fantasy that his future wife might think fondly of him; he is "unable to imagine the total negation in another mind of the emotions that are stirring in his own."[31] If this is what life looks like when one has genuine empathy for others—when one can truly feel what it is to be another— why should we encourage empathy? In seeking to explain this fissure, some point to Eliot's biography, insisting that the novella was written in a moment of personal crises. But more recently, critics have begun to take on questions of the relationship between knowledge and sympathy more directly. Kate Flint asks, "If sympathy toward others is a desirable thing, is it only possible to express this sympathy when we do not know as much as it would be possible to know about the other person?"[32] Flint concludes by noting that in *The Lifted Veil,* Eliot counters the Victorian desire of making all things visible by instead "arguing that we perhaps would not want to see where we might be able to see," privileging the imagination over the scientific eye.[33] Rae Greiner and Thomas Albrecht follow Flint by adding shades to the conclusion that Eliot's depiction of sympathetic extension in *The Lifted Veil* is in line with, and not in opposition to, her larger ethical project. Albrecht suggests that through a complex treatment of characters, the invocation of visual metaphors for other-awareness, and its indictment of Latimer's solipsism, *The Lifted Veil* is consistent with Eliot's broader conception of ethical engagement, an engagement predicated on the apprehension of difference.[34] I would go further to suggest that *The Lifted Veil* not only champions a selfless apprehension of alterity (an ability that, as Albrecht notes, Latimer lacks) but also places grave importance on learning.[35] It is too easy for Latimer, who gains his ability to see others' thoughts as a result of an illness. He thus assumes access to others in ways they cannot contradict, shutting down any possibility for surprise, and ensuring that even his engagement with a supernatural ability to experience another's reality is ultimately rendered a function of himself.

The recognition of radical alterity that Eliot endorses must be predicated on hard work: the hard work of earning literacy, and the pain of bumping up against the other's desires, experience, and consciousness. The ability always to anticipate the other precludes that collision. This is true of Eliot's characters just as it is true of Eliot's readers, and the glory of Eliot's work is that it shows a movement into that kind of awareness-of-limits which must precede intersubjectivity. That movement is not sufficient, but merely necessary, as some actors (Hetty, Rosamond) will retreat from their encounter with alterity and resume life—or death—as it had been. But others are able to effectively incorporate a newly nuanced understanding of the other into their lives—this is the work that enables Adam, Dinah, and Dorothea to end the novels facing a promising vista of potentiality.

CHAPTER 3

Thomas Hardy's Narrative Control

The Knowable and the Unknowable: Text and Character

What must a character do to deserve the label "the nastiest little bitch in English Literature"?[1] Sue Bridehead, in *Jude the Obscure* (1895), earned the distinction by, among other things, railing against social institutions of marriage and religion, refusing to be defined by conventional gender roles, and thwarting Jude Fawley's desire for her. But she is remarkable not only for her defiant posture; Sue's character actually upsets the narrative structure of *Jude the Obscure* by frustrating readerly expectations, expectations that are often aligned with Jude's. She usurps the title character of his central position, and she replaces that stable central role with her slippery, irreducible persona. Jude cannot understand or know her, but neither—it seems—can the novel. Hardy's well-documented fascination with Sue demonstrates his investment in the mystery that defines her character.[2] The mystery, in fact, generates the novel's driving desires: the wish to be heard and to understand is as powerful as the wish to tell and to be understood, both of which, as notes Peter Brooks, are "never wholly satisfied or indeed satisfiable."[3] Sue's character, and its articulation in *Jude*, coalesce a trend present throughout Hardy's fiction: her "inconsistency and elusiveness" mirror the formal idiosyncrasies of his texts.[4]

Sue is but one of Hardy's many inscrutable characters, but she in particular provokes intense critical scrutiny. Her elusive nature has led innumerous critics to pin her down, to make her consistent if only by explaining the source of her inconsistency.[5] Some suggest that the ambivalence of women's position in Victorian society is reflected in

Sue's emotional ambivalence and uncertain social status. Rather than an instance of incomplete or inconsistent characterization on Hardy's part, his inclusion of uncertainty surrounding Sue's character indicates the author's embrace of and grappling with those ambivalent social expectations. Hardy documents Sue's weirdness. He can, and does, describe her actions, but he also documents other characters' frustrations with her. She does confounding things, and not only do other characters remain confounded by her, but the omniscient narrator—ostensibly able to clarify Sue's motivations or intentions—further fails to offer clarification. Perhaps critical frustration is due to the sense that readers do not know more about Sue than Jude or Philloston know, thus complicating readerly pleasure. The described instability of Sue's character, her inscrutability, reifies a sentiment, an approach that pervades Hardy's fiction. Characters' scrutability is often contested within his novels, and it is precisely *within* the novels that Hardy establishes the difference between a character and the story of his or her life: the split between the knowable text and the unknowable person exists not only for the reader of the novel but also within the novel itself. That is, for Hardy's characters, one's self cannot be conflated with one's story. While personal narratives can be learned, molded, told, and retold, the individual other is and must always be essentially out of reach.

In *Jude the Obscure,* Hardy's final novel, Jude Fawley knowingly grapples with the impossibility of reconciling the mutability of Sue's character with his own desire for stability and sureness, but it is a maddening task. Even so, Jude views Sue's variability as one of her charms, at least in the beginning of their acquaintance and even as his personal delight in her borders on possessiveness: "His Sue's conduct was one lovely conundrum to him" upon their first outing together in Melchester, when he also thinks himself lucky that "only himself knew the charms" that her plain dress kept hidden.[6] He acknowledges that she is a "conundrum," but still relishes his ownership of knowledge of her that others do not or cannot share—Sue is "his Sue." Jude is thus ambivalent, but the fact that he even attempts to appreciate Sue's own ambivalence makes him unique among Hardy's leading men. Characters in Hardy's universe more often refuse to apperceive the instability of the other, clinging instead to a stable narrative about the other that they have constructed. Angel Clare, for example, develops an understanding of Tess that becomes concretized. When she reveals her past, he feels it as a violation not because she has wronged him, but because her narrative contradicts *his* narrative of her.

Not surprisingly, because these misunderstandings often occur between couples, much of the analysis of intersubjectivity in Hardy's fiction focuses on the ways that characters function as platforms for gender constructions. From attempts to define the author's apprehension of gender roles, wholesale pronouncements emerge: John Kucich, for example, concludes that Hardy's works show "a more negative interpretation of the inflexibility of female dishonesty in desire, or an excessively stark delineation of feminine dishonesty," while his male characters act as a "theater of charged moral ambivalence that can lead to resurgent moral purity, either through self-resistance or through resistance of the deviant examples of other, vilified men or of unregenerate women."[7] With such readings, immutable gender differences become a way to organize Hardy's characterizations, when in fact they are inherently fluid. Gender binaries can in these readings overwhelm the more subtle distinctions that Hardy draws between and among his characters. Gender cannot be set aside in any consideration of the relationship dynamics in Hardy's fiction, but refocusing on the way characters engage with alterity, it becomes clear that relationships with narrative, as opposed to fixed gender differences, determine intersubjectivity. The reader's desire to cotton on to definitive gender roles in his fiction is indicative of anxieties generated by the general instability of the Hardy narrative, wherein even those aspects of life that seem ultimately concrete are instead open for interpretation or alteration—gender, parenthood, family, religion, and inherent morality may all be unstable.[8] Even the past itself cannot be depended on, but is open for revision, interpretation, and reinterpretation.[9] As we will see in this chapter, one reason for this instability is that Hardy sets the novel in tension with characters' desire to view the past as solidified and booklike.

In this chapter, I focus primarily on two of Hardy's novels, *The Mayor of Casterbridge* (1886) and *Tess of the d'Urbervilles* (1891), to explore the ways that his works delineate those objects that *can* be appropriated by the self from objects that *cannot* be appropriated. Those that cannot are other individuals; instances of radical alterity can only arise, and necessarily arise, in one's encounter with another person. A story, much like a book, can be appropriated and is eminently knowable—the human other cannot be appropriated and is not ultimately knowable. By entrapping fellow creatures in static narratives, Hardy's characters defy that logic, essentializing fellow creatures and denying them sovereignty. The inability to engage in mutual or productive relationships, a sad circumstance so often featured in Hardy's stories, arises from a denial of alterity, a consequence of turning the unknowable other into a knowable narrative. This distinction is different from the recognition of a disparity between reality and a story that a character believes; such distance between lived experience and a dream world no doubt figures prominently in realist fiction, but it cannot account for the alterity of the other. Hardy goes beyond merely exposing the "discrepancy between the inner narrative and the novel" by insisting that neither an individual character's construction of reality nor the novel itself can adequately contain the other;[10] he uses stories to point toward the distinction between narratives and the people they describe.[11]

In this way, Hardy's novels demonstrate a truism at the heart of Levinasian ethical philosophy: the other is always unknowable, and recognizing that limitation is necessary to positive affective relationships. What's more, as the human other is the ultimate limit of knowledge, all other things—including narrative—are fungible, assimilable. This construction works against the desire of so many literary critics to make the object of their study—the text—an ethical agent on the order of the human. Teasing apart these manifestations (the fictional character from the material novel) is difficult even for critics devoted to ethical criticism. In her Levinasian readings of Victorian literature, Jil Larson falls back on an all-too-common movement of ethical literary critics: "The act of reading a literary character, of experiencing literary art, is fraught with some of the very same paradoxes and difficulties of establishing a just and loving relationship with another human being, and that is why art's potential to be ethically instructive is as strong as its potential to shelter us from the real and the ethical."[12] Levinas in particular explicitly cautions against this collapse.[13] Hardy's works help to provide a corrective against that collapse by insisting on the difference between story and self. His novels exploit this disconnection to great effect: showing always that when people make the same mistake critics do, assuming that a person's story is somehow analogous to the person herself, no real apprehension of alterity can ensue. Again, this is an impulse routinely modeled in realist fiction: the text, the aesthetic object, is fixed and appropriable (as much as a novel might depict the exigencies of ethical dilemmas and decisions, it offers only that representation). It is explicitly not the other. Hardy echoes this distinction within his novels; some of his characters continually rail against aligning themselves with the permanence of text and are instead fluid, mutable, capricious, and mercurial, while others embrace the stable narrative too fully, refusing to accept or acknowledge inherent mutability, often to disastrous effect. Men *and* women, Hardy reminds us, are not books.

The Mayor of Casterbridge: *Reading the Past*

The human inclination to cling too tightly to the stability of a fixed narrative is fleshed out in *The Mayor of Casterbridge* (1886). Michael Henchard's obstinate embrace of the past dooms his business and personal relationships with men and with women; his is not only a portrait of hubris or chauvinism but also a portrait of a stilted reading and poor interpretation. A fundamental lack of human control underlies many of the events of the novel, which depend as much on the vicissitudes of the (nature-controlled) grain harvest as they do on the actions of any character.[14] To whatever extent *The Mayor of Casterbridge* is a document of rural Wessex farm and labor culture, it is also a portrait of the individual's ability to negotiate with the more abstract powers that control his life, and the desire to seize upon other humans as powers that may be controlled.

Michael Henchard owns a past that is condemnable. Whereas Tess will be guiltless or at least guileless in her seduction by Alec d'Urberville, Henchard bears full responsibility for selling his wife and young daughter at a country fair. He was drunk, but that drunkenness is represented not as an excuse for his actions, but as merely one in a series of ill-advised choices. Henchard's decision sets into motion a plot that seems at first to endorse the possibility of change, as Henchard repents of his actions and the drunkenness that contributed to those actions and starts anew; he rises successfully to become the mayor of Casterbridge after abandoning his past life.

Hardy signals the obstacles that change will play in the narrative by first placing the reader in a position that, like Henchard's, is challenged by change. He opens the novel with Henchard's most shocking act—the auctioning of his wife—with little background to contextualize the action. The reader is thus immediately confronted with Henchard's least likeable qualities: his coldness, his drunkenness, and his impulsivity lead to an impression that is difficult to shake. So while the novel presents a story of change, Henchard (like the reader) only experiences the new movements of his life against the backdrop of his unshakeable belief in the permanence, the petrifaction of his story. *That* dependence, that clinging to a narrative even in the face of evidence that life choices might redirect the narrative in all directions, decides Henchard's fate. Even while disavowing his past, he grants it a permanent place in his mind; believing his success to depend on the complete repression of the life he led, he ensures that the past is always with him. His sobriety is itself only a respite from his default of drinking, a temporary bandage on a permanent affliction, as Henchard returns to drink once he completes the twenty years he had pledged to sobriety as penance for his actions. When confronted with the irrepressible physical reality of his wife and daughter, he tells no one of their shared past, refusing to believe that anyone would hear this story and not render the same scathing judgment that he renders himself. His desire to be unknown even in death confirms this intractability regarding the past. Henchard is doomed by his dedication to a narrative that need not have been the defining feature of his life; he is doomed by his staunch belief that the story makes the man.

Henchard's rigid conception of the life story is seen in his own life, but it is in relation to others that it becomes clear that he grants *no one else* the flexibility or forgiveness that he denies himself. His relationship with Farfrae held the promise of business success and friendship, but the specter of Henchard's past overwhelms that possibility. The wages of stolidity are even more pronounced in his relationship with his presumed daughter Elizabeth-Jane, which held the promise of shared affection and even devotion, though he proves unable to enter into that mutuality. She would willingly have devoted herself to him, yet he remains "the bitterest critic the fair girl could possibly have had."[15] Among the many differences between Elizabeth and Henchard is the way each understands the past. For much of the novel, Henchard knows Elizabeth's past when even she does not, a fact that he attempts to exploit. Elizabeth must then reconcile multiple versions of her life story throughout the course of the novel, first believing herself the daughter of Richard Newson, then the daughter of Henchard, and then back to Newson.

Concerned as Henchard is that others might uncover or discover his past, it is not surprising that the terms that define his relationship with Elizabeth are terms of reading: handwriting, books, and reading faces, all of which Henchard views as interpretable clues of a fixed reality. He is keenly attuned to reading features, as are many in Hardy's oeuvre, where, as Jonathan Wike concludes, "the face is the natural point of convergence of the symbolic and the existential, the meeting place of the man behind it and the world beyond it."[16] Henchard's appraisal of Elizabeth-Jane while she sleeps offers certainty that he is not her father but rather that Richard Newson (the man who purchased Elizabeth's mother) is, and the information is unbearable:

> He steadfastly regarded her features. They were fair: his were dark.
> But this was an unimportant preliminary. In sleep there come to the
> surface buried genealogical facts, ancestral curves, dead men's traits,
> which the mobility of daytime animation screens and overwhelms. In

the present statuesque repose of the young girl's countenance Richard Newson's was unmistakably reflected. He could not endure the sight of her, and hastened away. (124)

And so he can see "unmistakable" evidence of her background. Why should his past be any less readable? More important, in this scene Henchard offers the readers evidence of his inability to escape himself. His response to Elizabeth is negative; if others might read his transgressions as easily as he reads her parentage, would their responses be any less negative?[17] He forecloses the possibility that the other might surprise.

Elizabeth-Jane, the subject of Henchard's scrutiny and the recipient of one act of astute "reading" on his part, serves as a useful counterpoint to his rigid intellect and self-conception. Her mother was introduced as having a singular attraction—the "mobility" of her face (4). It is hardly a conventional compliment, yet in Hardy's oeuvre, there are few physical commendations greater than mobility. Sue Bridehead's eyes are "liquid," her face "mobile, living" (89, 90); Tess Durbeyfield has a "mobile peony mouth," Angel's face and mouth are "mobile" as well.[18] Elizabeth-Jane is her mother's daughter (though expressly not Henchard's), and she is gifted with a quick and flexible mind to match the "mobility" of her expression.[19] In the quotation above, it is clear that Henchard views such mobility as a "screen" that "overwhelms" the genealogical facts of the face, which are more like *geo*logical facts to Henchard, evidentiary, fixed, and interpretable.

While Henchard interprets Elizabeth-Jane's physical features in order to conclude that he was not her father—a version of reading nature's syntax not unlike those detailed in George Eliot's fiction—Hardy complicates the theme of literacy to distinguish between the father and daughter. Despite his accurate interpretation of Elizabeth-Jane's face, Henchard's interpretive powers are otherwise inferior to hers. Partly because Elizabeth sees literacy as a means to effect change, her interpretative ability creates a space for mutability and, through the practice of learning, the recognition of the limitations of her comprehension. Elizabeth's literacy not only marks her as Newson's daughter as opposed to Henchard's (she uses her father's money, after all, to purchase books), but it calls attention to the greater, nongenetic, differences between her and Henchard. In Henchard's harsh critiques of the girl, the split between the two becomes clear, and Hardy's narration counters Henchard's assessment through more positive diction. For example, Henchard, considering himself a member of the "truly genteel," regards Elizabeth's use of dialect as a "mark of the beast," while the narrator describes her use of dialect as "occasional," "pretty," and "picturesque" (127). In one episode, described as "a gratuitous ordeal," Elizabeth is made to write out a contract agreement for Henchard and a visitor. In this passage, language, reading, and writing become inextricably linked with personal identity—Elizabeth-Jane is an "omnivorous reader," yet for Henchard, her handwriting (like her dialect) serves as another undeniable, legible sign of her inferiority to Henchard, the man she believed to be her father. Her script, described by the narrator as "a splendid round, bold hand of her own conception, a style that would have stamped a woman as Minerva's own in more recent days," is considered by her father to be a "line of chain-shot and sand-bags" (127). He becomes embarrassed and, "in angry shame," decides to write the agreement himself (128). This is not Hardy's only invocation of Minerva, the goddess of wisdom, in relation to Elizabeth-Jane; she is later described as having an "incipient matronly dignity, which the serene Minerva-eyes of one 'whose gestures beamed with mind' made easy" (318). Yet Henchard is fixated on a past that expected something else from a woman's pen; his focus on the historical past blinds him to the possibility of change in the present. Further, he "believed that bristling characters were as innate and inseparable a part of refined womanhood as sex itself" (that recalcitrant gender definition, one way that he traps Elizabeth-Jane in an unalterable narrative) and instead of being proud or recognizing Elizabeth's value, he "reddened in angry shame for her" and dismisses her from the room (128). Henchard may hew to strict gender roles, but that does not mean that Hardy does, a distinction that is missed if Henchard's behavior is put down entirely to his being a man during a certain historical moment.

Elizabeth-Jane's reading and writing indicate her ability to understand what others cannot, and she is thus able to make links between the parts of stories that others miss, a fact that comes to bear most significantly in her relationship with Lucetta Templeman, Henchard's fiancée. Lucetta, like Hetty Sorrel, understands that she is read by others around her, and seeks to control her countenance in order to control their readings: she asks a mirror, "How do I appear to people?" (173). Yet even Lucetta's awareness does not mean that she can completely control the ways she is perceived—proper "reading" depends as much on the skill of the actor as on the skill of the interpreter (think, for example, that Michael Henchard is able to discern accurately Elizabeth-Jane's parentage *only* when she is asleep, and thus has no control over her expression), and Elizabeth proves to be a discerning interpreter of Lucetta's desires: "The rencounter with Farfrae and his bearing towards Lucetta had made the reflective Elizabeth more observant of her brilliant and amiable companion.[. . .] [S]he somehow knew that Miss Templeman was nourishing a hope of seeing the attractive Scotchman. The fact was printed all over Lucetta's cheeks and eyes to any one who read her as Elizabeth-Jane was beginning to do" (170).

Elizabeth-Jane's mode of interpersonal engagement is one of two versions established in *The Mayor of Casterbridge*. Both require interpretation and comprehension of signs, symbols, texts, and stories; but whereas Elizabeth-Jane leverages her literacy to create new spaces for intellectual growth or deepening awareness of those around her and to undermine the fixed narratives in which she finds herself, Henchard is fixated and fixed with regard to others as well as himself. The ways that each individual negotiates the past is reflected in the ways that each negotiates those present others. Living in constant fear of his own past, a narrative that threatens his present only because of the power he invests in it, Henchard applies a similarly rigid mode of reading to others. It takes in little, and in its fixity, views others in terms of fixedness, conflating story with identity, eliding potential in favor of conventional expectations. Elizabeth-Jane's fluid mind, much like the mobility of her expression, grants to others a similar fluidity. Though both she and her father do, in places, discern others accurately, Elizabeth-Jane uses her interpersonal literacy to distinguish between the individual and the story. Henchard's insistent fixity follows him to his very grave. He attempts to determine, through writing, the ways others will view him even after death, stipulating in his will that "no man remember me" (321).

In *The Mayor of Casterbridge*, these two approaches to understanding one's story—as fixed permanence or as a narrative always under construction—lead to very different results. It's curious that Henchard does end up miserable, dead, alone, which might be precisely the end one could anticipate given his uninspiring opening gambit. Between the novel's beginning and end, Hardy shows readers that Henchard's end is a consequence of closing down the other, trapping him in a fixed, impenetrable narrative. Those same lessons evolve in *Tess of the d'Urbervilles*.

Faithful Representation: Tess of the d'Urbervilles

From the first page of *Tess of the d'Urbervilles*, the nature and function of stories and storytelling are questioned; the novel opens with Parson Tringham telling John Durbeyfield the story of his aristocratic ancestry.

The novel's dynamics seem to be determined by the retelling of that tale: Tess tells it when attempting, at her family's insistence, to "claim kin" with the d'Urbervilles; she hides it while working at the dairy; and she does, finally, tell it to Angel Clare. And the provenance of the Durbeyfield name is only one of the narratives of Tess's life. To tell or not to tell becomes a central concern of the novel, and Tess herself becomes defined, to large degree, by the version of her life's story people believe about her. Within the novel, there is no stable version of reality, but always multiple stories, multiple iterations, multiple renderings. And as the actions that unfold depend on which variation of the past is known, and often with little regard to an empirical notion of truth and reality, the novel seems to suggest that what matters—the thing that determines actions and reactions—is the story or stories that one believes. That story may be learned and is knowable, while the characters that inhabit the story remain always elusive. Here, then, the acts of reading, interpreting, and understanding narrative collide directly with the empathic project of reading, interpreting, and understanding the other: they are not, Hardy consistently reminds his readers, the same project.

One version of Tess's story is the one "told" by her body, a natural story of beauty, youth, and purity that seems to contradict her experiences of, for example, the shame of rape and stigma of unwed motherhood. The novel's subtitle, "A Pure Woman," calls into question that physical narrative. On one hand, her body does tell the story of her purity; on the other, it is also that body that was seduced, that killed, and that bore a child. The seeming contrast between her body and her life leads to others in the novel reaching "contradictory and deceptive readings" about Tess's character.[20] Her body is, throughout the story, read as one thing when it is really another; she is read as older and more mature when she is in fact young and immature, and it is read as virginal when she has already given birth to Alec's child. Must only one reading be correct? Nature might seem to be an author that one cannot refute, but in fact it too offers no single, accurate reading. When Tess is young and truly an innocent to the ways of the world, her voluptuousness renders her appearance like that of a woman far older and far more experienced than she is. This fact can be manipulated, as Mrs. Durbeyfield does when dressing Tess for her journey to meet the d'Urbervilles. Notably, Tess does not dress herself, but is a passive participant in the process: Mrs. Durbeyfield washed and brushed Tess's hair, adorning it with a "broader pink ribbon than usual"[21] and "put upon" Tess a dress that "imparted to her developing figure an amplitude which belied her age, and might cause her to be estimated as a woman when she was not much more than a child" (49). Such social signals rely, as Joan Durbey-field does, on all viewers understanding what she intends. Clothing Tess in ribbons and mature dresses, Joan co-opts nature's syntax.

If Tess's body tells changing stories, it is only right that her readings of others or of situations are similarly whimsical. Flexibility, mutability, capriciousness are not, it must be noted, uniquely positive qualities, a fact that makes *Tess of the d'Urbervilles* a progression from *The Mayor of Casterbridge*. Tess's flightiness does not always serve her well. For Tess, in spite of her relative innocence, is aware that she has become the object of the gaze of others (her mother's being a relatively benign instance), a prospect that at times she intuitively guards against. Know-ing not only that she is stared at but the implicit danger in such stares, "though sometimes her journey to the town was made independently, she always searched for her fellows at nightfall, to have the protection of their companionship homeward" (64). Here, Tess takes the active position of working to safeguard her body, aware that it is interesting and "graceful" (64) and, moreover, *young*. Tess is not always so active, and other times she abdicates her agency to the whims of her mother and—perhaps as a result—she blames Joan Durbeyfield for the results of that abdication. Though she will not walk home alone at night, Tess does not know to seek protection against Alec; or, rather, does not seek that protection. Her decision seems at first to be warranted, as Tess is described as being "mentally older than her mother," and she dismisses Joan's plans for her marriage to Alec as meaningless. Yet Tess later admonishes her mother for *not* informing her about the potential con-sequences of visiting the d'Urbervilles: "Why didn't you tell me there was danger in men-folk? Why didn't you warn me? Ladies know what to fend hands against, because they read novels that tell them of these tricks; but I never had the chance o' learning in that way, and you did not help me!" (82).[22] Joan has no response equal to Tess's accusations, but is only "subdued."

The relationship between Tess's character, as defined by the choices she makes and her experience of those choices, and the version of her character as it is understood by her family, co-workers, or lovers, is unstable at best. In some cases, as in the example above, Tess accurately reads the intentions of men who leer at her from dark corners, and steels herself accordingly. In other instances, as in her encounter with Alec, she is either unaware of the consequences of her choices or knowingly puts herself in danger and then protests her ignorance. In still other instances, she overanticipates others' response to herself, believing that she is being harshly critiqued by her fellow townspeople when she is not. In fact, Hardy writes, her worries are "founded on an illusion" that others scrutinize her when, in fact, "She was not an existence, an experience, a passion, a structure of sensations, to anybody but herself." The fear that generates "misery" is due to her cultivation of the "conventional aspect" as opposed to "her innate sensations" (91). At times she interprets accurately, at times she interprets inaccurately, and at times she does not interpret at all. Tess's varying acuity this area argues against Tess's being "constructed" solely by or through the gaze of others; not only are her interpretations inconsistent, she is in no position to judge the relative accuracy of her interpretations. Tess's other-construction is limited by her apprehension of others, just as others' constructions of Tess are limited by their own apprehension of her. Despite or perhaps because of the intense attention paid to Tess's physical beauty by both the novel and its characters, she remains curiously *strange*. Kaja Silverman frames the problem nicely: "the very density of this representational activity attests to the difficulties of containment—to a certain slippage of Tess out of the paradigms that structure her."[23]

Tess's ambivalent relationship to her family's history mirrors the multiplicity of her physical narrative. At times, she works against the claim to ancestry that led her to Alec, having "no admiration" for her ancestors, and instead "almost [hating] them for the dance they had led her" (102). (One of her finest qualities is her beauty, and the narrator notes that it obviously comes from her mother and is "therefore unknightly, unhistorical" [20].) Tess worries that a single, definite version of her history—such as that defined by genealogy—will rob her of her individuality and remind her that her nature and "past doings" "have been just like thousands' and thousands'"(126) that came before her. Tellingly, Tess describes this concern by calling to mind the fixed, permanent narrative of a book: "What's the use," she asks Angel, "of learning that I am one of a long row only—finding out that there is set down in some old book somebody just like me, and to know that I shall only act her part; making me sad, that's all" (126). The fixed narratives of books limit the potential for change and preclude mutability. Wishing *not* to be "set down in some book," she disavows her own history. Instead, she creates another, alternative narrative, equally tantalizing to Clare. Realizing that his interest in her was "largely owing to her supposed untraditional newness" (128), she cultivates a lack of tradition, a lack of convention, essentially a pastless, storyless existence that is expressly counter to those made permanent by writing.

In this way, Hardy uses the novel form to underscore the disconnection between *its* solid permanence and the fluidity of the people described therein. *Tess,* like most of Hardy's longer narrative fiction, leverages the *most* rigid formal qualities of the novel. Hardy's difficulty in choosing the title for *Tess* is a telling example of his concern: he rejected numerous versions before alighting on his final choice, and the oscillation shows a hyperconcern that it be right.[24] Chaptered, titled, chronological, the novel's plot and structure buttress Tess's accounts of the fixedness of books.[25] By allowing Tess, whose survival depends on her ability to control her own narrative, to critique the unbending stability of the written word, Hardy demonstrates the ambivalence afforded by his position as author: he is on the one hand the person who makes narrative permanent, and on the other hand the person who may attest to the impossibility of fully concretizing a person.[26]

The tension between story and experience—between the fixed and the in-process—is most vividly rendered in Hardy's depictions of lovers. J. Hillis Miller described romantic relationships in Hardy's oeuvre as "loss of self-possession";[27] lovers' "ceaseless moments of longing" are driven not by "simple desire for possession of another" but, he suggests, by a "desire for something else which seems to be accessible by way of the beloved."[28] Miller argues that Hardy's characters seek self-fulfillment through the beloved,[29] but this result is often thwarted through a character's "failure to obtain the woman he loves" or "by his discovery that he does not have what he wants when he possesses her."[30] I argue that the relationships are doomed because the desire is, from its inception, solipsistic. Clare, perhaps a typical Hardian male, understands the beloved not as a separate being whose presence would complement his own, but instead as always already a construction of himself. Another Hardy protagonist, Edred Fitzpiers of *The Woodlanders*, acknowledges this limit when he admits to Winterbourne, "I am in love with something in my own head, and no thing-in-itself outside it at all" (115). And the most extreme example in Hardy's oeuvre is Jocelyn Pierston from *The Well-Beloved* (1897), a sculptor on a quest to find the living female incarnation of his personal and artistic ideal.[31] Angel Clare—like these men—discovers not, as Miller writes, that "he does not have what he wants" once he wins his beloved, but that what he wanted all along was a version of himself.

To wit, Tess's insistence on rejecting a stable, bookish version of her past is based on her (possibly projected[32]) belief that Angel would prefer such blankness and freshness. Indeed he seems to, but his understanding of people, of others, is in fact built on utterly rigid conceptions, wherein he cannot allow an individual room to change or even deviate from the narrow narrative he has fixed upon him or her. Tess's blank past becomes a screen onto which Angel can project himself, though Clare cannot see his influence. Once Tess appears to him, her story—which he problematically equates with *her*—becomes fixed and fetishized; Clare functions by concretizing the flexible and historicizing the fresh. When faced with any information outside of his version of Tess, Angel simply cannot reconcile the two. Hardy's metaphors for this process depend on natural imagery of solid metal: "Within the remote depths of his constitution, so gentle and affectionate as he was in general, there lay hidden a hard logical deposit, like a vein of metal in a soft loam, which turned the edge of everything that attempted to traverse it. It had blocked his way with the Church; it blocked his way with Tess" (241). Clare's position is complicated by his *seeming* awareness of Tess's individuality—that vein of metal exists within the otherwise "soft loam" of his expansive mind. Tess's appreciation of this awareness serves as a primary source of his pain. He seems, according to the narrative, to note and respect her individuality, characterizing his "conscience" as that part of him that recognizes her "precious life": "a life which, to herself who endured or enjoyed it, possessed as great a dimension as the life of the mightiest to himself. Upon her sensations the whole world depended to Tess; through her existence all her fellow-creatures existed, to her. The universe itself only came into being for Tess on the particular day in the particular year in which she was born" (154). Still, his convictions mean little when challenged, and his actions in light of difficulty prove to be unequal to those stated beliefs. The contrast between Clare's statements and Clare's actions calls further attention to the disconnection between text and life illustrated throughout *Tess*.

If Angel presents a combination of rigidity couched among proclamations of free-thinking flexibility, his understanding of Tess presents an equally complicated vision. He believes her to be simple in her desires and expectations: he thinks, "what a creature of moods she was, and how careful he would have to be of her when she depended for her happiness entirely on him" (196). Even here, her mercurial moodiness does not preclude her complete dependence—whatever her mood, then, her happiness always depends on Angel. Is this an indication of his solipsism, that even when accounting for her variability he reduces her to a constant? In other moments his understanding of her as being dependent on himself, however, is shown to be incomplete. The narrator adjusts the reader's impression of Clare's version of Tess a few pages later: "Clare knew that she loved him—every curve of her form showed that—but he did not know at that time the full depth of her devotion, its single-mindedness, its meekness; what long-suffering it guaranteed, what honestly, what endurance, what good faith" (213). Here, "single-mindedness" and "meekness" ensure that "endurance" and "good faith" define Tess's love; these are, at best, ambiguous qualities of a lover. Clare understands her to be dependent on him for her happiness in the present, but is apparently unaware of how persistent her devotion is (note as well that enduring devotion *to* Clare is not the same as complete dependence *on* him).

So while he may not grasp the depth of her dedication, and while he recognizes her mutability, Clare does believe Tess is knowable.[33] His persistence and rigidity become paramount when Tess confesses her past to him. Now, faced with information that he cannot reconcile with his version of her, he rebels, insisting that she (the fixed, the dependent) is fundamentally altered. His language after her confession is stark. When she notes that she forgives his own earlier transgressions, he responds, "Forgiveness does not apply to the case. You were one person; now you are another. How can forgiveness meet such a grotesque prestidigitation as that?" (228). Critics seized upon Hardy's choice of words here, noting that "prestidigitation" was hardly the *bon mot* many in Angel's position would choose.[34] Yet the word is telling, planting Angel firmly in the ground of the bookish, the stolid, and the unmoving, even as he accuses Tess of being a shape-shifter. One hoped-for result of Tess's telling her past is the creation of a vision of the other that is commodious enough to contain multiplicity; she seeks to open out her own narrative to include coexisting versions of self—the Tess who carried Alec d'Urberville's baby is the same Tess who stands before Angel. If she wishes to connect her past to her present, it is through an incarnation of personal history that insists on the unknown and multiple; she does not seek to construct a stable, single, "historical self."[35] The revelation of her past has so altered Angel's perception of Tess that he wishes to alter *other* parts of her past so that her story better fits the embodied Tess he sees before him: in his mind, the actions of the person must match his narrative of that person, even if doing so requires changing the narrative he clings to. Curiously, this does not reflect a propensity to adapt. Clare simply rejects entirely the old narrative and creates a new one (which he treats as if it were *always* true) that conforms to present events. Tess's noble ancestry at one point stood for her worthiness; now, he says to her, "I think that parson who unearthed your pedigree would have done better if he had held his tongue" (232). While that story may be altered or may be wished never discovered, nature's writing poses an even greater challenge. It is through Angel that Hardy articulates most directly the frustration wrought when nature's syntax proves to be untrustworthy.

Angel is continually nonplussed by such discord. He is "stupefied" and argues "erroneously" with himself, trying to reconcile her transgressions with what he believes is the uncontestable story told by her beauty (235).

Clare's recalcitrance would then seem to leave him ill-equipped to engage in fruitful relationships, but he ends the novel alive, hand in hand with Liza-Lu, the "spiritualized image" of Tess. Tess ends the novel in death, that most fixed, stonelike state. One might read these ends as just rewards for their lives—Tess punished for her crimes and Angel living on with the potential for future happiness as recompense for his trials. But the novel's dynamics demand that death be recognized not as a predetermined, eternal punishment but rather as the ultimate unknowable state, a state for which Tess is remarkably well adapted. In willing Liza-Lu to Clare, Tess acts upon a most intimate comprehension of Angel's desires without compromising her own. If Henchard's will, requesting that "no man remember me," manifests his last attempt at controlling others' encounter with even his memory, Tess's final request manifests her acute understanding of Angel's desire (as opposed to her own) for continuity. In Liza-Lu, she intends Angel to have what he seems to want most: an incarnation of Tess that revives his early mental constructions of her—as Tess describes it, "all the best of me without the bad of me." Her final utterance to Angel, her final line recorded by the novel, "I am ready," then shows her resignation to (or welcoming of) the unknown.

This circumstance arises to varying degrees throughout Thomas Hardy's fiction; the wages that conflicting narratives inflict on interpersonal relationships are central to his plots. By layering those personal narratives within the novel's discourse, he ensures that the metanarrative reflects a similar tension: having access to a narrative—any narrative—does not ensure access to the person it details. Much of the conflict that his characters experience arises when they, or others around them, cannot reconcile their lived experience with the narratives describing, and thus defining, that experience. Despite Tess's desire to create a present that does not depend solely on her past for meaning, Angel's response to that desire inhibits her ability to transcend her past with him. It's not just what you've done that counts; it's what others think you have done. Tess thus remains unknown and unknowable to Angel; her inability to anticipate his reaction to her revelation (an inability, but certainly not a fault) ensures that he remains unknown and unknowable to her. He cannot grant her independence from his apprehension of her. And while it might seem that the greater fault lies with Angel than with Tess, the novel makes clear that blame is a meaningless pursuit.

The Novel and the Face-to-Face

With his characters, Hardy interrogates the terms with which individuals encounter other individuals, and the role that narrative plays in those encounters is unmistakable. To confine an individual to a narrative is to make that which cannot be known (the human) into that which can be known (a story). By insisting on that distinction within his novels, Hardy makes explicit what was more subtly present in Dickens's and Eliot's[36] works: the final limitation of the realist text, a limitation that is essential to the realist project, is that the text can never fully account for, explain, or contain, the human individual. That limitation does not inhibit productive representation; it enables productive representation.

The novel, both its material manifestation of bound paper between two covers, and its less tangible version—the story it details, the words chosen to detail that story—are thoroughly and eminently knowable. They can be plumbed, torn apart, analyzed, and memorized: they can be consumed, in short, by a reader. Consumption serves a useful parallel here, in that it connotes the act of a reader bringing the novel into her own self. But, and here is where Hardy's work in particular becomes a useful illustration of the idea, since the novel can be consumed by the reader, the reader cannot admit its radical alterity. That is, to return to Levinas's useful formulation, there can be no face-to-face with a novel. It is the people who inhabit the novel who retain their alterity only in relation to the other characters within the novel. Hardy's works iterate and reiterate the disconnection between the individual and her story, between the man and the narrative of his life, by depicting problems that arise when the two are collapsed. When one person refuses to recognize the alterity of the other through the consumption or reification of the other's story, the possibility of effectual affective relationship ceases to exist. It is only in the granting of autonomy, the acknowledging that he cannot know her through her story, that any movement forward is possible.

When Hardy's characters think about others, they think about the narratives that define those others—actions, genealogy, pasts, physicality. That his novels themselves replicate this relationship, offering the reader a narrative that describes and defines the characters within, might seem natural. His contribution to lessons of empathic engagement arises in his constant devotion to upsetting those narratives—diegetically, Hardy shows that no stable definition can contain an individual but that instead the person always exceeds any limits defined by narrative. His characters are not reducible to their stories. Pulling back, his novels themselves uphold this argument by straining at their own boundaries:

Sue's slippery character, Tess's series of unenviable bad luck, Henchard's preternatural stubbornness. To uphold the dynamics that define his argument, Hardy suggests that his novels exceed his grasp in moments, and they seem to; that excess calls attention to the often fraught relationship between form and content—trying to represent that slipperiness within a novel casts into relief the permanent materiality of the novel form itself. That relationship, as will be seen in the next chapter, becomes a central concern in James McNeill Whistler's painting, in which inscrutability becomes a subject as well as a style.

CHAPTER 4

Learning to See

Whistler's Visual Aversions

An image of the Chelsea pier at night, a Nocturne (figure 2) in misty blurs of gray, is so small—only 8 by 10 inches—that it demands that viewers approach closely; yet even close scrutiny offers little definitive pictorial information. No objects or landmarks are discernible, and the dock's edges, if indeed that is what they are, are only hinted at with specks of red amid the field of silvery blue. There is modulation in the color; the image is interesting and complex, but it defies viewers' attempts at interpretation. A drypoint from 1861[1] adopts a different pictorial vocabulary, eschewing the blurred diffuseness of the Nocturne in favor of black hatches of color, but achieves a similarly unwelcoming effect (figure 1). It depicts a solitary male figure with his back to the viewer. He faces a window, its six panes divided by heavy black lines, the central mullion cutting into the middle of his head. He sits in a ladder-back chair; its horizontal slats are barely discernible in the print. Driving toward him are all directions of scratchings, each line bearing the burred, inky edges of Whistler's drypoint technique.

Neither of these works by Whistler is particularly inviting. The Nocturne is unfocused and foggy, and its content is explicitly and emphatically muddy. The figure in the drypoint refuses the viewer's attempt to interpret or engage through his position (his face turned away in the image) and through elements of the composition that intrude between the man and audience. The cross-hatching common to all etching here mimics and amplifies the barriers between subject and viewer, barriers that include the ladder-back chair, the window mullions, the edges of the table and bench, and the beams that line the ceiling—all of these elements simultaneously point to the figure and block him from view.

These two images—one a landscape and the other of a single subject—distance their audience with visual obstacles.

In another category of Whistler's oeuvre, group scenes depict individuals with barriers between them, as opposed to or in addition to the interpretive barriers between viewer and image. Here are people sharing a space, a room, a conversation, a family, a moment. And yet Whistler's pictorial strategies insist on the subjects' disconnection, even alienation, from one another, all without undermining artistic verisimilitude. Through this insistence, Whistler accomplishes a feat parallel to that of the realist authors: he depicts images of people that are profoundly moving, yet profoundly unreachable, all the while emphasizing through form the necessity of connection. This chapter focuses on three of Whistler's earliest canvases—*At the Piano* (1858), *Harmony in Green and Rose: The Music Room* (1861), and *Wapping* (1860–64)—to explore two of Whistler's techniques for capturing these moments of disconnection, fixing them permanently on the canvas: the use of profile and deliberate obfuscation via pictorial cluttering. These techniques form part of the repertoire of Whistler's painterly methodology and philosophy.

I shift to Whistler's painting as a means of demonstrating the trend in nineteenth-century realism to emphasize the unbridgeable alterity of the human other. In doing so, I anticipate one vociferous objection: Whistler's work has little in common with realist painting, much less with realist fiction. Indeed, Whistler's diffuse, idiosyncratic style might appear to reject the tenets of realism espoused by his contemporaries or the authors addressed in this study; the techniques of alienation Whistler adopts in his painting actively and expressly resist, for example, narrativizing. And yet, Whistler's very resistance to narrative links his works to those of the realist authors. His painting emphasizes the formal aspects, the painterly qualities of painting that make the work of art a spectacle, while frequently resisting the spectacularization of the human subject. The visual aversions that could seem only to alienate the viewer are actually quite productive; his paintings, much like Hardy's novels, draw a clear and unmistakable line between the work of art itself, which is knowable, and those figures depicted within those works, who are not knowable to one another. In addition to that distinction, Whistler develops an intricate visual language, with which he depicts interpersonal dissention, discomfort, or alienation. The insistent disconnectedness of those depicted within his paintings signals a fundamental lesson of Victorian realism: even in gatherings of intimates, the human other remains always ultimately unknowable.

Whistler may present viewers with images *of* inscrutability, but his canvases invite analysis, focusing the gaze of the viewer on his method of representation. It is a distinction Whistler himself insists on. One may not be able to identify the exact location from which Whistler painted the Chelsea pier; one may not be able to discern what time of day or night a scene occurs; one may not know who—as in the case of the etching—a figure represents. But by eliding identifiable markers of content, Whistler shifts the weight of his works onto their form. When viewers jettison anxieties associated with content labeling, the modulations of color, technique of paint application, even the size of the canvas, all readily discernible qualities, move to the foreground. Those knowable qualities remain in tension with the murkiness of the scenes or relationships depicted. His titles reflect a will to obscure; his mid-career decision to title or retitle his paintings using musical terms was surely influenced by Aesthetic and Symbolist trends, but at its base was less an act of fidelity to an artistic movement than a means to deflect viewers' attempts to narrate the images he paints. Perhaps more than the other realists addressed in this study, Whistler is alive to the fact that letting go of expectations of comprehensive certainty is difficult for readers or viewers, and his attempts to manipulate viewers' expectations with regard to both form *and* content may be felt as perverse.

Despite this rich fodder for analysis, his oeuvre has remained until very recently remarkably underanalyzed and undertheorized. As recently as the 1990s, critics bemoaned the lack of critical attention received by Whistler's work in comparison to the wealth of attention devoted to his biography.[2] One reason for the omission is that his life story is easily as interesting as his work; he was equally provocative in both, his highly idiosyncratic behavior matching the unicity of his artwork. One recent critic breezily summarizes the public Whistler as follows: "a pugnacious but dandified American expatriate aesthete, precocious champion of Japonisme, quick-witted and sharp-tongued battler of the press, painter of 'Nocturnes,' 'Symphonies,' and 'Arrangements,' beyond whose surface lie barely perceptible traces of recognizable motifs."[3] The Whistler of this description—Aesthete, dandy, rabble-rouser—is but a cartoon version of the real, complicated artist, but a cartoon so compelling that even the very reductive biographical sketch often overwhelms consideration of his art. Some of the blame for that reductive portrait must fall on Whistler himself, who was not always savvy—or was perhaps too savvy—about the attention he sought. Whistler's self-promotion reached what some regard as an apotheosis in his broadly publicized 1878 libel trial against John Ruskin. Whistler published his account of the trial in a volume titled *The Gentle Art of Making Enemies*; the title alone shows the artist's wry disdain for his critics.[4] This moment, and the style of

Whistler's painting that was at the heart of the civil action, becomes the touchstone for Whistler's oeuvre.

Given the idiosyncrasies of his life and self-promotion, it is not surprising that when recent scholars turn their attention to Whistler, they turn to his later works, works in the style that inspired Ruskin's sharpest criticism. There are two results of this focus: first, by emphasizing his later, London-based work, such criticism encourages a portrait of Whistler defined within and against a strongly British art environment. Second, because the criticism emphasizes Whistler's later (British) work to the exclusion of his earlier work, Whistler's oeuvre appears to have more in common with that of Albert Moore and Frederic Leighton than with the works of French realists *or* with the artists described by Tim Barringer as "Hogarthian barbarians of mid-Victorian art": William Holman Hunt, William Powell Firth, and Ford Madox Brown.[5] Whistler emerges, in contrast to those moralistic painters who valued verisimilitude in representation, as an Aesthete.[6] Elizabeth Prettejohn—writing in what might rightfully be considered a definitive text on Aesthetic art—acknowledges the painter's ambivalent position within the Aesthetic movement, noting that Whistler was not "a spokesman, self-appointed or otherwise, for an artistic movement that might be united under" the "art for art's sake" slogan, conceding that his work, and the theory to which his work contributes, "is nonetheless exemplary for the range of practices that explored the question of what art might be, if it were for the sake of anything else."[7] Ultimately, though, she situates his eccentric, nonnarrative work firmly within the Aesthetic tradition, citing with approval Colvin's description of the works of Whistler, Leighton, and Moore as "beauty without realism."[8] Even those reevaluating Whistler's work cannot escape the claim of Aestheticism: Rachel Teukolsky makes the case that Whistler's Aesthetic drive links his work to the modernism that follows, but does not engage the earlier link in that chain, the French realist tradition in which Whistler trained.[9]

Whistler's prominence within the critical literature on Aestheticism ensures that his place in the development of realist iconography is overshadowed by French painters. Michael Fried rightly includes Whistler among the "Generation of 1863" in his *Manet's Modernism*, but his is a lonely voice;[10] no work of Whistler's appears in Linda Nochlin's seminal (and heavily French) *Realism*, which focuses on France during the period of Whistler's tenure there. That the artist's biography precludes a stable identification, national or otherwise, contributes to the issue. Born in America, Whistler traveled extensively, trained in France, and settled in London with his sister and brother-in-law. Unlike Mary Cassatt, for example, who left the United States but firmly inserted herself into the French art scene, where she longed to stay, and did indeed stay, Whistler was peripatetic. Moreover, his timing was odd: he moved from France to Britain at a time when French art was exploding in new directions and British art was, by comparison, conservative if not reactionary. Whistler and his art seem to fit comfortably into neither the French nor the British art-historical traditions. While he was in France, Courbet was his teacher, and it is in Courbet's realist tradition that Whistler cultivated his early treatment of figures and developed his unique pictorial language. He might later have rejected the influence of Courbet on his work ("il n'y en a pas eu, et on n'en trouvera pas dans mes toiles," he writes to Fantin-Latour in the late 1860s) but the resonances are evident.[11] Whistler was grounded within an existent and emerging movement; the variations in representational strategies that would define his artistic individuation from that movement were influenced by and manifested in response to a uniquely French realist tradition, which he in turn influenced.

Whistler's contribution to that realist tradition exhibits a movement out of and away from the perceived teleology of Western art—his style (and, unlike many of his realist contemporaries, his life) extends past high realism into the twentieth century, when his refusal to engage in narrative painting does align him in some way with those anti-realist Aesthetes. His later work, especially, seems to fall out of that juggernaut of ever-increasing verisimilitude, driving always to eliminate "those obstacles which impede the reproduction" of an external, universal reality.[12] The assumption that art drives always to greater verisimilitude has long been assailed by art historians,[13] just as its literary complement has been assailed by literary critics, yet it remains remarkably resilient, and any consideration of realism in text or images must still be divorced from claims of objectivity. Whistler's realism resides not in the objectivity of his images but rather in what he chooses to represent and how he does so, and foremost among his contributions to realist iconography is his pictorial insistence on the surface of the painting, his refusal to encourage narration of images, his depiction of interpersonal discord, and his use of a variety of techniques to obscure access to the individuals represented in his paintings. It is precisely these modes of representation, techniques that might feel alienating to a viewer accustomed to more conventional (Victorian) paintings with more conventional (Victorian) messages, that form the central focus of this study.

Whistler's insistence on the formal qualities of painted images, including the habit of referring to his paintings as "arrangements," confounds the viewer and art historian. About the portrait of his mother,

Prettejohn summarizes this reaction: "we are forbidden, apparently, to speculate on the character, biography or feelings of the sitter, and told peremptorily to consider her merely as an 'arrangement.'"[14] Though Prettejohn notes the upside to Whistler's instruction—that in describing the painting as an arrangement, the artist frees the viewer from the influence of his own emotions, predilections, or expectations—she does not quite consider what happens when we *do* regard Whistler's paintings as arrangements. What do the arrangements tell us—the bifurcated scenes, the solid verticals cutting up the interiors, the emphatic verticals breaking up the spaces between the paintings' subjects? In objecting to a traditional moralizing, Whistler opened up the way for something else—a means of painting that explicitly depicts its subjects as unique individuals, insistently making those subjects unknowable to the others who share the canvas. And through that depiction, the artist shatters the viewer's access to the safety of a unifying narrative, and offers instead a meditation on the fiction of understanding the other.

Realist Bona Fides

Early in 2009 an exhibition of the domestic scenes of Nabis painter Pierre Bonnard opened at the Metropolitan Museum in New York. Bonnard's intimate spaces, often centered on a dining table or a window, frequently feature human figures who appear coldly at odds, a curious effect considering the warm tonal glow of what look like cozy spaces. Drawn mostly from Bonnard's late period from the mid-1920s through the 1940s, the images seem, as some critics have noted, to engage stylistically much more with the artistic past than with the period during which they were painted. Bonnard's artistic style feels more comfortable among earlier Vuillards, Cézannes, or Gauguins than it does among his late contemporaries Picasso or Matisse. What then locates his works in the Modernist tendencies of his period are his scenes of interpersonal alienation, what Christopher Benfey calls "domestic disturbance, isolation, and sadness."[15] Still, the sense of shared discomfort that does appear thoroughly contemporary has its roots in a realist—a nineteenth-century—past. This mode of representation, as Benfey accedes, places Bonnard's interior scenes among the works of Ibsen or Henry James. Through that earlier realist genealogy—from Gauguin and Cézanne backward to Manet and Courbet—one can locate the genesis of the temperament communicated in Bonnard's uncomfortable, though beautiful, interiors. In particular, the depiction of discomfort between people within their everyday milieu must be located in a realist ancestry. And one essential component of that French family tree is Whistler.

Among the novel choices deployed in French realist paintings was the representation of disharmony, and one way to depict misunderstanding was through seemingly alienated subjects; communal scenes were one trope representing nonidealized, ostensibly nonposed, rural life. Illustrating community is not as simple as depicting a group, a problem regularly explored in Courbet's works.[16] Courbet's *Burial at Ornans* (1849–50), for example, includes some forty-five figures, seemingly representing an entire community. Despite its size (over 10' x 20') and breadth of subject choice, it does not depict communal *unity*, but rather "internal tensions and ambiguities," and what T. J. Clark called "collective distraction."[17] This depiction of a crowd that seems comprehensive, cutting across class boundaries, attending an event that might be regarding as unifying (a burial),[18] appears instead as a scene of people mired in their separation and well aware of their differences from one another.

Even outside of large-scale communal scenes, subjects with disparate body positions, effaced from one another or the viewer, can denote miscommunication. Édouard Manet was Whistler's cotemporary, and in his oeuvre the trope is prevalent, and is, indeed, regarded as a hallmark of his style. That Manet is among the *most* analyzed artists of the period makes him an interesting complement to Whistler. Manet's *Le Chemin de Fer*, for example, features a woman and child, and while the woman is situated directly facing the viewer, the young girl's back is turned toward both the woman and the viewer.[19] The woman's dog is unconcerned with the viewer as well. That one subject *does* gaze directly out of the image negates the reading that the subjects were captured unawares or spontaneously (as often happens in, for example, Degas' works). Such paintings suggest a world in which the subject may seem to be aware of his viewer and may seem even to acknowledge his viewer instead of his companion. *Le Balcon* (1869) is another example of such an image in Manet's oeuvre, as are *Argenteuil, Déjeuner sur l'herbe* (1863), *Olympia* (1863), *Nana* (1877), and so on. That those people depicted within the immediacy of the frame of a painting should somehow *miss* each other is much like the situations within the examined novels, where proximity never guarantees connection. The representational tropes that these canvases share, defying as they did conventional iconography, did not ingratiate their viewers, and a negative critical response should, perhaps, have been expected.

Manet's thwarted and problematic connections with his audience are another trait he shared with Whistler. Manet's tortuous relationship with the Salon judges, his critics, and his public attests to the power of his signifiers being interpreted in ways he did not expect. The audience's insistence on narrativizing the images he painted was one source for their hyperbolic reactions, as the narratives (as opposed to the paintings themselves) provided the basis for many of the objectives. The public furor over *Olympia* (1863) demonstrates this idea, and certainly Whistler, working and exhibiting at the same time, experienced the risks of this kind of painting and the pitfalls associated with the narratives provided by viewers and critics. Manet's painting was thrust into a world that constructed meaning out of readable markers, and class seems to be inscribed in the trappings of the image, including the title: "*Olympe*," Nancy Locke writes, "was a pseudonym in use among nineteenth-century prostitutes."[20] Just as nature's syntax may be read on the face of a perfect beauty, it may also, the argument goes, be read on the face of the prostitute. T. J. Clark argues that the most readable aspect of *Olympia* is her nakedness, though critics were unable to deal with this fact because of the "lures" of the image that detract attention away from the body: "the cat, the Negress, the orchid, the bunch of flowers, the slippers, the pearl earrings, the choker, the screen, the shawl—they were all lures, they all meant nothing, or nothing in particular,"[21] a fact that did not stop critics from interpreting those red herrings innumerous ways. If one accepts Clark's argument that the objects in the image signify nothing, that lack of signification was itself provocative. *Olympia* refuses, in a sense, to be read within the comfortable confines of art criticism or social drama.[22]

Whistler's *The White Girl* (1862; later renamed *Symphony in White No. 1*), a rare case of his painting a woman in full face, was displayed in the 1863 Salon des Refusés with Manet's *Déjeuner sur l'herbe*. Like *Olympia*, *The White Girl* goaded critics *not* to supply a narrative, a challenge they failed miserably.[23] Yet unlike Manet's works of the same period that have received near constant critical attention, *The White Girl*, "no less ambiguous than Manet's [works], has remained relatively undiscussed."[24] The prettiness of Whistler's canvases distinguishes his work from Manet's, but he shares with Manet the knack for creating images that resist narration.

The Trouble with Reading

From the French realist tradition Whistler gained appreciation for images of discord and a potentially antagonistic bent for disappointing spectators' desire for the comfort of narrative certainty. French realism also provides example after example of images that, after initial critical derision or apathy, went on to be hailed as exemplary if not genius works—and as Whistler would outlive many of his realist cohort by decades, this trend bolstered his willingness to persist stubbornly against naysayers. Whistler had, by the 1860s, moved to England, where the general tenor of the visual arts remained moralizing and narrative-based, rather than embracing the French trends toward a new visual vocabulary defined by Courbet, Manet, and others. Pamela Fletcher notes that "a test of aesthetic success" of any painting was its "ability to arouse emotion in its viewers," and the proper result of the desired emotional response was a movement toward moral edification if not direct altruistic action.[25] Viewers, as Whistler wrote, seemed to confound beauty "with virtue," asking before paintings, "What good shall it do?"[26]

Whistler had good reason to critique that conflation of morality with aesthetic judgment. While in France even the academic establishment was by this time beginning to embrace the possibilities of representing images outside of narrative and outside of communion, in Britain the Academy was still rewarding paintings that implied narrative as well as morals. In fact, there seemed to be a causal relationship between an implied story and an implied moral; see, for example, Millais's *The Order of Release*, Hunt's *The Awakening Conscience*, or any of the biblically or mythologically inspired works of the Pre-Raphaelite Brotherhood. The libel trial against Ruskin solidified the position of Whistler's works within a binary conflict "between literary, moralizing art identified with Victorianism and the purely pictorial, self-referential aesthetics associated with nascent modernism."[27] But the struggle began long before the trial. Augustus Leopold Egg's *Past and Present* triptych (1858) is one work typical of "literary, moralizing art identified with Victorianism." Egg illustrates three scenes that Ruskin understood as the unraveling of a marriage ruined by a wife's infidelity. In each, the symbols for marital disharmony are so obvious that they nearly cease to be symbols.[28] The first, hung in the center, depicts a woman prostrate on the floor in front of a man, wringing her hands. Two young girls sit in front of a collapsing house of cards, which had been built upon a novel by Balzac (of course). An apple is sliced in two: one half sits on a table next to the husband and is stabbed by a knife. The other half is on the floor, lying next to the wife. To Ruskin, these images spelled out a narrative with utter certainty; he summed up the narrative told by the other two canvases of the triptych in his exhibition review: "the husband discovers his wife's infidelity; he dies five years afterwards. The two lateral pictures represent the same moment of night a fortnight after his death. The same little cloud is under the moon. The two children see it from the chamber in which they are praying for their lost mother, and their mother, from behind a boat under the vault of the river shore."[29] Even outside of the specificity of Ruskin's supplied narrative, the paintings unmistakably represent misery, and the title *Past and Present* suggests a causal relationship between events depicted in the first canvas and the sadness that permeates the second and third. It is perhaps not too great of a leap to conclude that Egg intended to communicate a moral: adultery will be punished by misery for all involved. In reading this story *into* and *onto* the image, Whistler believed, the qualities of the image are ignored. Little riled the artist more.

In *Ten O'Clock*, an 1885 lecture that was later printed, Whistler defined the problem with this approach—often prescribed by the mediating critic—to "reading" paintings:

> For some time past, the unattached writer has become the middleman in this matter of Art, and his influence, while it has widened the gulf between the people and the painter, has brought about the most complete misunderstanding as to the aim of the picture. For him a picture is more or less a hieroglyph or symbol of a story. Apart from a few technical terms, for the display of which he finds an occasion, the work is considered absolutely from a literary point of view; indeed, from what other can he consider it? And in his essays he deals with it as with a novel—a history—or an anecdote. He fails entirely and most naturally to see its excellences, or demerits—artistic—and so degrades Art, by supposing it a method of bringing about a literary climax. It thus, in his hands, becomes merely a means of perpetuating something further, and its mission is made a secondary one, even as a means is second to an end.[30]

First, Whistler critiques the act of looking for an invented unknown beyond the image instead of regarding the surface of the painting. Far from proposing a theory of art that depends on a pure superficiality, that is, an art that lacks *depth,* he is countering the Ruskinian tendency to compose extended narratives that usurp the primacy of the image. Whistler refocuses on the surfaces of the canvas so that it resumes its position as fundamental and not secondary to the story it purportedly tells; the canvas must not be appropriated by moral claims, and it should not function merely as a vehicle for a lesson. Whistler is not arguing against analysis or interpretation, but against the unnecessarily and formulaic pasting of a narrative onto what is expressly *not* a narrative.[31]

That Whistler's rejection of Ruskinian tendencies focuses on the approach to appreciating a work of art rather than on the content, per se, of a painting becomes clear when we consider Ruskin's adoration of Turner. Turner's later work has much in common with Whistler's—the diffuse and suggestive landscapes, the lushly imprecise depiction of natural elements—but while Ruskin wholeheartedly champions Turner's works, he routinely denigrates Whistler's. On one level, the distinction is due, as David Craven writes, to Ruskin's perception of the "vulgar commercialization" attributable to Whistler's "willful deletion of associative values" in an attempt to gain wealth "without contributing to the betterment of society."[32] Yet even when Ruskin praises Turner on seemingly purely visual or formal terms (as opposed to narrative, commercial, or moral ones), it is because Turner's works inspire "associative thinking,"[33] making demands on the interpretative powers of the viewers. Ruskin felt, as Elizabeth Helsinger describes, that Turner's canvases made "greater demands on his viewers" while at the same time providing explicit direction. To the extent that Ruskin recalls the "familiar romantic interest in the unfinished or incomplete," he praises Turner because of the "precise directions for imaginative activity" that his paintings provide.[34] Whistler's refusal to offer instruction through titles (where a great contrast between Whistler and Turner's work can be drawn) and his statements about art and criticism seem to foreclose all interpretative acts.

Curiously, in his effort to distinguish his images from narrative, Whistler nevertheless outlines an approach to art that is analogous to that of the realist writers. Whistler proposes in his own work a means to counter the symbolic and chronological pictorial elements that seem to compel narrative readings of images. It is not a new critical approach as much as it is a new compositional approach.

One consequence of Whistler's admitted distaste for the moralizing aspect of much conventional Victorian visual art is that he is, as I have noted above, too often aligned with others who spoke loudly against the conventional—the Aesthetes. Despite his adherence to a belief that art should be regarded (seen) for its own merits and demerits as opposed to its instructive value, his version of rendering art must not be conflated with the Aesthetic dictum "art for art's sake"; further, it is important to note that he was not universally regarded as an Aesthete even in his own time. Wilde accused him of "[explaining] to the public that the only thing they should cultivate was ugliness, and that on their permanent stupidity rested all the hopes of art in the future,"[35] and of loving the ugly, finding *"le beau dans l'horrible."*[36] This particular criticism was not new to realist artists, who since Balzac had been accused exactly of a fascination with or adoration of the ugly and base. For Whistler, the charge sits uneasily because of the very prettiness of his imagery, if nothing else. In fact, that surface beauty allows other critics to charge Whistler with the opposite: rather than fetishizing the ugly, some suggest, Whistler instead "aesthetically and psychologically evade[s] concern for the human dilemmas rife in east London and [. . .] even nullif[ies] these dilemmas by subsuming them into his overriding aestheticism."[37]

Indeed, much of the scholarship on Whistler and his oeuvre insists on its prettiness, often to the exclusion of analysis of technique or composition. Whistler's regular and highly idiosyncratic use of the profile in his compositions, for example, garners little attention. In Roy McMullen's biography of Whistler, the trope earns merely a glancing mention and is explained away as a means to render his subjects in a most flattering position. Describing *At the Piano* (1858), McMullen includes Whistler's penchant for the "profile view that idealizes a sitter" among his other traits: "an association with music, a preference for muted light, and a readiness to be pensive."[38] The idealizing of a subject, preferences for one kind of light, and pensiveness are qualities of the artist, of course, and not necessarily the art, and McMullen's aim is to construct a biography, not art criticism. In other cases, even the expectation of prettiness can be overwhelming; nearly all discussion of his iconic portrait of his mother, *Arrangement in Grey and Black,* insists on equating his representational choices with lack of emotion; it is described as "decidedly unsentimental"[39] with colors that "are low key, verging on monochrome" and as a "composition" with " the willful oddity of a harshly cropped Polaroid"[40] when in fact the image simply does not conform to a typically Whistlerian aesthetic of diffuse softness. If the lack of prettiness causes viewers to read more discord in an image that it demands, when images are too pretty, viewers risk overlooking discord altogether.

Repeatedly, though people share the frame, they do not seem to share an experience. Compared with others' works, the difference in Whistler's group depictions is stark. Consider again Egg's *Past and Present;* it too depicts discord, but while its subjects might not share a gaze, they certainly are actors within the same space, responding to the same events—a posture that is not frequently discernible in Whistler's works. A more salient comparison might be one made by Elizabeth Prettejohn, who compares Leighton's *Spanish Dancing Girl* (1867), Moore's *A Musician* (1867), and Whistler's *Symphony in White #3* (1865–87) to illustrate their shared traits. In Leighton's and Moore's paintings, there are multiple subjects; in Leighton's, as the title indicates, a Spanish girl (later, the painting was renamed *Greek Girl Dancing*) dances while three onlookers clap, and in Moore's, two lounging women listen to a man playing a lyre. The settings of both paintings seem to be classical—all subjects wear the loosely draped clothes of the ancients, and in both paintings all of the subjects are sharing the experience of listening to the music produced within the painting. One might safely assume that the Spanish (or Greek) girl is dancing to music supplied by someone outside of the images, and at the very least the clapping of the three people watching her would provide a rhythm; in Leighton's, there can be no doubt that the man is playing the lyre. Other than the title, there is no indication of music *within* Whistler's *Symphony in White #3*. Moreover, Whistler's painting clearly depicts women in contemporary dress—it is a scene influenced by the japonisme that Whistler encouraged in his interior design; it is a Victorian scene. Here, as elsewhere, the choice of title is not intended to give the viewer insight into what is happening within the scene; we are not meant to view the painting as a scene of two women sharing the experience of listening, for example, to a symphony. Further, the two women in Whistler's painting, though sharing a space, are posed in direct contraposition. The woman on the divan leans with her back to the sitter on the floor, her legs forming a vertical barrier between the two. Though their arms reach out toward one another, they do not touch. It is, in other words, a scene of disconnection, of averted gazes, and of physical dissimilarity. Prettejohn collapses these distinctions to claim that the three paintings are of a piece, are all examples of high Aestheticism. I would suggest that despite their superficial similarities—similar color tones, a similar softness of rendering—the three paintings reflect the fundamental difference between Whistler's work and that of the Aesthetes: his painting depicts contemporary subjects, resists on every level a narrative, and gestures toward the interminable alienation between people.

At the Piano: *Family in Profile*

In this earliest of Whistler's successful canvases he sets down the artistic vocabulary that will define his oeuvre: the use of elements of the scene to separate subjects from one another and the depiction of subjects in profile. The visual space of *At the Piano* (figure 3) is defined in stark geometrics: the bisected bottom halves of two frames split the upper half of the image and are themselves split. This break is continued through the dual black piano legs. These vertical elements create a central separation that separates mother from daughter.[41] Echoing the upper horizon of the piano is that most Victorian of decorative elements, the wallpaper dado. Just as the two frames break the image up into two parallel columns, coinciding with the two figures, this horizontal similarly breaks the visual plane into upper and lower sections: the sitters' heads are severed from their bodies. The result is a grid of four quadrants, balanced via opposition or repetition in shape and color: the mother's black triangular body to the daughters' white triangular body, the larger frame picture behind the smaller girl, and the smaller framed picture behind the larger mother. Even the girl's shoes repeat the bracketing-off—their black straps crisscross against her white tights. Visually, it appears as a sort of mathematic equation, and on both sides are appropriate Victorian versions of mourning.[42]

Breaking the plane this way ensures that a viewer realizes the spatial distance between the two figures as well as the figurative distance between them. It also mimics the spatial separation of the stereoscope, what Jonathan Crary calls "the most significant form of visual imagery in the nineteenth century."[43] In what was then a popular diversion, two subtly different images are blended via the prismatic lenses of the stereoscopic viewer to give the viewer the illusion of a three-dimensional vista. Without that technology to blend the images, to mimic the human eye's depth perception, a viewer can focus on only one of the images at a time, the left *or* the right, but not both simultaneously. Whistler's manipulation of this two-halved image insists on the *lack* of depth in his picture space. There is an emphatic lack of blurring, lack of mingling possible. Contributing to this effect of flat space is his use of expanses of color: the mahogany of the piano, the white of the girl's dress, the black of the mother's dress, the green that is repeated in the dado on the wall and the shadow of the seemingly empty frames.

As McMullen notes, Whistler employs the profile for both women, yet the organization resists McMullen's reading that the arrangement flatters; rather, it obscures. Further, though they face each other, the subjects are not looking at each other, as might be expected in such a composition: the viewer regards the right side of the mother's face and the left side of the daughter's—they are placed facing each other; the mother plays the piano, the daughter ostensibly listens. And yet even that connection, one playing what the other hears, is not at all obvious. The mother's head is turned downward and inclined slightly to the right, and her focus seems to be the keys beneath her fingers. The child faces straight ahead and yet, because she leans against the piano at its bend, is not directly across from her mother and cannot be looking directly at her. Also separating the figures from one another are the markedly different techniques and styles used on their faces, contrasts that echo the other contextual juxtapositions of the image. The crisp, reflective surface of the piano's top contrasts with the softened, nearly muddled rendering of the girl's face.[44] Warm-toned and fresh, she lacks the pictorial specificity of the older woman's features, whose wrinkled face and double chin render her features discernible and readable in comparison.

In this early work, Whistler places two women in close physical proximity. They appear to be family. They appear to mourn a single person. They appear to share a moment of music, one playing and the other listening. And yet the composition insists on representing barriers between the two. These barriers are both physical, like the piano separating the women from each other, and visual, like the hard vertical and horizontal lines defined by the frames images, the dado, and the piano leg. Even the solidity of both women's skirts seems repellent; all in all, it is an image of shared space but not of shared experience.

Harmony in Green and Rose: *Crowded Scenes and Cross-Purposes*

If *At the Piano* represented an isolated instance of these tropes demonstrating pictorial disconnection, the glosses of gallery notes or biographers might suffice to explain Whistler's choices. But it is not an isolated instance; the strategies are repeated over and again, comprising the phonemes on which his artistic vocabulary is built. *Harmony in Green and Rose: The Music Room* (1861) (figure 4) features two of the same sitters depicted in *At the Piano*, Whistler's sister and his niece, and it continues the trend begun in *At the Piano*. *The Music Room* also anticipates the pictorial moves that will come to define those who follow him: the mirror reflects a face effaced—present but not pictured in the primary frame of the image; a mirror does not reflect those figures that do occupy the focal space; visual space is flattened to the degree that the figures appear to be collaged cut-outs from other paintings. The image raises the same questions as *At the Piano*—are these three female figures experiencing the same moment in the same space?

Whistler achieves the effect of separation in a surprisingly cluttered scene. Whereas *At the Piano* was defined by austere horizontal and vertical splits, in *The Music Room* those orthogonal lines persist but are joined by the effusive floral of window drapes that both reinforce the vertical lines, repeated as they are four times throughout the image, and scatter the cleanly readable right angles that, in the earlier canvas, composed the matrix that defined the pictorial space. And yet, just as the harsh angles of *At the Piano* enforced the rigidity of the separation of the two figures through their solidity and impenetrability, here the tangled mess of flowers (modeled on the actual drapes of the artist's sister's London house[45]) contributes to the claustrophobic feeling of the image as a whole.

For *The Music Room* illustrates another version of disconnection, one predicated on too-closeness as opposed to separation or distance. The figures crowd the image, quite literally. The woman in black in the foreground overlaps the young girl reading. Pushed off the canvas on the left would be the figure whose face is reflected in the mirror—she is present, but only via image, her physicality rendered offstage. Those drapes function in this regard as well; not only their print but their placement indicates business and cramped space. They overlap the girl's dress, their reflection in the mirrors blocks the woman's reflection (and the reflection of the drapes is in turn blocked by the vase's reflection), they puddle onto the floor in excess. Whistler's aesthetic regard (or disregard) for the drapes notwithstanding, their contribution to the scene is essential. Countering the flat spaces of black and white defined by the dresses, the contrast emphasizes both extremes. Whereas in *At the Piano* those monolithic presences of mother's and daughter's dresses stood opposed and apart, here the black dress—not the mother's this time—intrudes onto the space of the daughter's dress. The curve of the woman's bustle suggests a further crowding. And the flattening of the space is used to particular effect in the contrast between white and black; there is so little communication between the images, one imagines that they exist in different picture planes.

The effect of crowded disconnection—of people crammed into a tight space and yet utterly unaware of the other or unresponsive toward the other—echoes Courbet's *Burial at Ornans*. Here Whistler achieves a similar effect: the women who are, ostensibly, facing one another are depicted as looking instead toward the same direction—both look to the left, one with her head inclined backward and the other forward. Splitting the two older women, the girl sits opposing each. She turns her face down, reading. If she were to be looked at, by mother, by visitor, or by viewer, she would not meet the gaze.[46]

The title is important too.[47] Whistler's penchant for musical names provokes a curious reflection: whereas *At the Piano*, which depicts a musical scene, does not benefit from a retrospective renaming, *The Music Room* does. It, like *At the Piano*, already evinces musicality in its title, even if there is no pictorial evidence of music in the scene. And yet "Harmony" as his choice—does it indeed call attention to the harmonious mingling of green and rose? Or is the naming ironic, as the image is hardly one of interpersonal harmony. Whatever narratives biographers may assign to the scene—the mourning visitation of a friend to the family, for example[48]—the painting is noisy, cluttered, and features three figures, none of which is seen in communion with any other. What kind of harmony is this?

Depictions of a lack of communication or lack of shared experience, of alienation, are represented by spatial distance but also by the cluttering of bodies, piling one on top of the other, glances effaced. It is as if Whistler insists on the distinctive presence of each figure, even going so far as to depict them in ways that make them appear as if they were not in the same space. Proximity, then, guarantees neither union nor communion.

Wapping: *Visual Interference*

In the later *Wapping* (1860–64) (figure 5), however, three figures *are* represented as sharing in a communal moment. Three figures sit around the table. Titled for the area of the London docks where Whistler was staying, it is a subject that he reproduced numerous times. The hatched lines of the boats' masts and rigging form a tight web, a confusion of lines that Whistler returned to again and again.[49] In *Wapping*, the mass forms the background for an intimate seated group, pushed to the forward boundary of the frame in the lower right corner. Art historians and biographers alike have named the sitters and provided narratives for the events depicted, usually describing a transaction between one of the men and the woman, a prostitute.[50] What Whistler has painted, however, explicitly illustrates a scene that comprises a number of the elements that defined his earlier sitting-room paintings, all of which resist narrative. Between the woman and the central man are interposed at least seven visual barriers: the five lines of the sail behind, the gray pole (presumably a mast) with a pulley, and the black column supporting the roof; between him and the man on the far right are more sail lines and the heavy, impenetrable frame of a window. Here, as in the refined London parlor, the image contains barriers. And here Whistler's insistence on the superficiality of the painting is crucial. Considering the image as a scene from a story, a photograph capturing a moment of everyday life, one could certainly argue that these lines do not separate the sitters, as the rigging, the mast, the column, and the window frame are all *behind* them and thus do not interfere with their communication. Visually, those elements function as barriers between the subjects. The window frame, for example, is not delineated by line, paint, or color from the blackish blur where the man's body might be.

Each of the three is painted in a curiously different manner, anticipating wildly different artists and echoing the differing manners of representation that distinguished the two subjects of *At the Piano*. The woman resembles Renoir's dappled portraits of Valadon, her hair casting a fuzzy reddish halo around her head and her mouth blurring into her face; the central bearded man suggests Manet's *Le Bon Bock* (1873), with ruddy skin, and clearly delineated lines on his face; and the second man, face suspended on a body cut out of the image, suggests blue-period Picasso, completely flattened, eyes hollow. Though the location has shifted, can we consider this grouping to be fundamentally different from the women in the drawing rooms of a London townhouse in *At the Piano* and *The Music Room*? They too are separated by representational style and by elements of the image that slice through the space they share.

Looking at, Not Looking through

Whistler's artistic philosophy can perhaps best be summarized in the distinction he draws between looking *at* art and looking *through* it. For literary critics who privilege interpretation, it might surprise that Whistler comes down firmly on the side of looking *at*. Yet Whistler's attitude is not that of the Aesthete; we should not ask that painting "elevate," but neither should the panel "merely decorate":

> Hence it is that nobility of action, in this life, is hopelessly linked with the merit of the work that portrays it; and thus the people have acquired the habit of looking, as who should say, not *at* a picture, but *through* it, at some human fact, that shall, or shall not, from a social point of view, better their mental or moral state. So we have come to hear of the painting that elevates, and of the duty of the painter—of the picture that is full of thought, and of the panel that merely decorates.[51]

In refusing to provide his audience with stable narratives that reinforce conventional notions of morality, Whistler forces that audience to encounter images which—through that very refusal—demand new ways of seeing. The artist shatters the viewer's access to the safety of a unifying narrative; he risks alienating his audience but gains an opportunity to create a new engagement with painting. Flattening the image field, embracing musical titles, gesturing at a sense of presence rather than the instillation of a narrative; these aspects define Whistler's oeuvre as does, perhaps, warring against the scenes of domestic tranquility that, for example, George Eliot marveled at in Dutch genre painting. Doesn't the suggestion that his canvases inscribe the similar disconnection on display in realist novels perform the same reduction of image to narrative? Am I not imposing a story—that Whistler seeks to represent difference—where he would instead prefer a response to the canvas as canvas? In fact, it is Whistler's very insistence, in his technique and composition as much as his statements (which depended constantly on sarcasm, irony, and provocation) on flatness, on the refusal to render images according to the strictures of true perspective and illusionism preferred by the neoclassicists who preceded him, that makes his work such a useful parallel to fiction. He insists adamantly on the artifice of his art, and not only in ways that align him with the Aesthetes. Art for art's sake is, after all, not the same as art that confines itself to presentation, and not representation. There is no ingratiating beckoning from the eyes of his women, no acknowledgment of the other figures *within* the frame, much less of those outside of it, that is, those in the viewer's position. Amplifying the artifice of the paintings, the artist reminds viewers that the thing is simply that: an object that, like the bearskin rug the subject stands on, can be moved, taken off the wall, reframed, or bought for two hundred guineas. It is consumable. Those he represents, however, are not. They are not consumable; they may not be captured or bought—not even in the images themselves; not even by the painter. Whistler's visual strategies defy the viewer's desire to see the painting as an instance of alterity. Like Hardy's fiction, Whistler's images insist that their subjects, and not the paintings themselves, are instances of the other. We may read his pictorial strategies as resisting interpretation, but in fact they call more attention to the fact of their paintedness. They instruct us to look at the paintings, and in doing so, what we see are images of people who are at odds, who are not looking at one another. Insisting that we look at and not through, he reminds that the painting is a thing.

These are aspects of painting that make it a compelling counterpoint to fiction. The unchangeable, unchallengeable boundary defined by the canvas's end (a boundary Whistler plays with, as in *The Music*

Room, reminding us of its presence and that it leaves some out just as it includes others) is analogous to the defined parameters of the novel, its first sentence serving as one boundary and its last sentence as the other. Proximity does not guarantee notice, or understanding, or recognition. Whistler's paintings depict inscrutability; so if they do mirror reality, they reflect the inscrutability inherent in all others. They show us that disconnection must be recognized and cannot be explained away; they capture dissention and concretize discord, all within and among a style that is unmistakably beautiful.

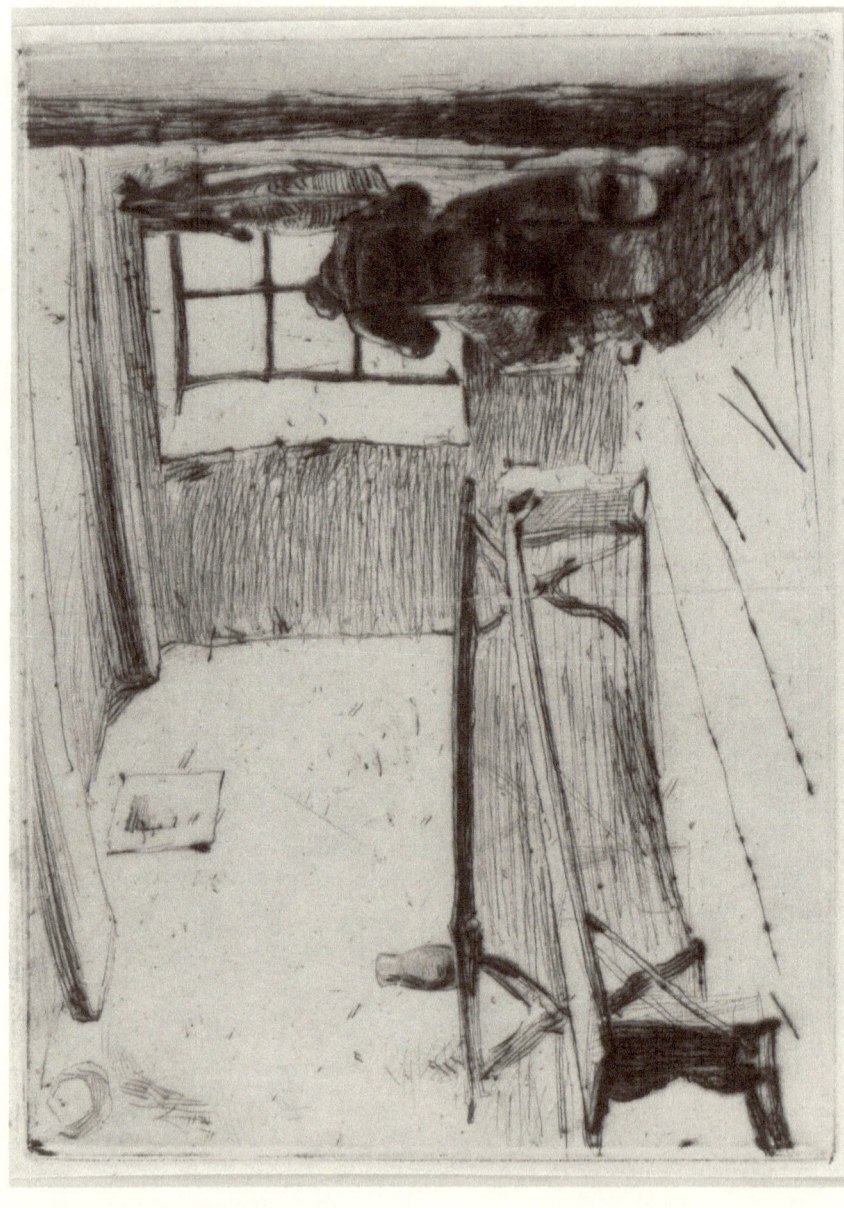

Figure 1. James McNeill Whistler, The Miser (1861). Drypoint on paper. Freer Gallery of Art, Smithsonian Institution, Washington, DC.: Gift of Charles Lang Freer, F1898.310.

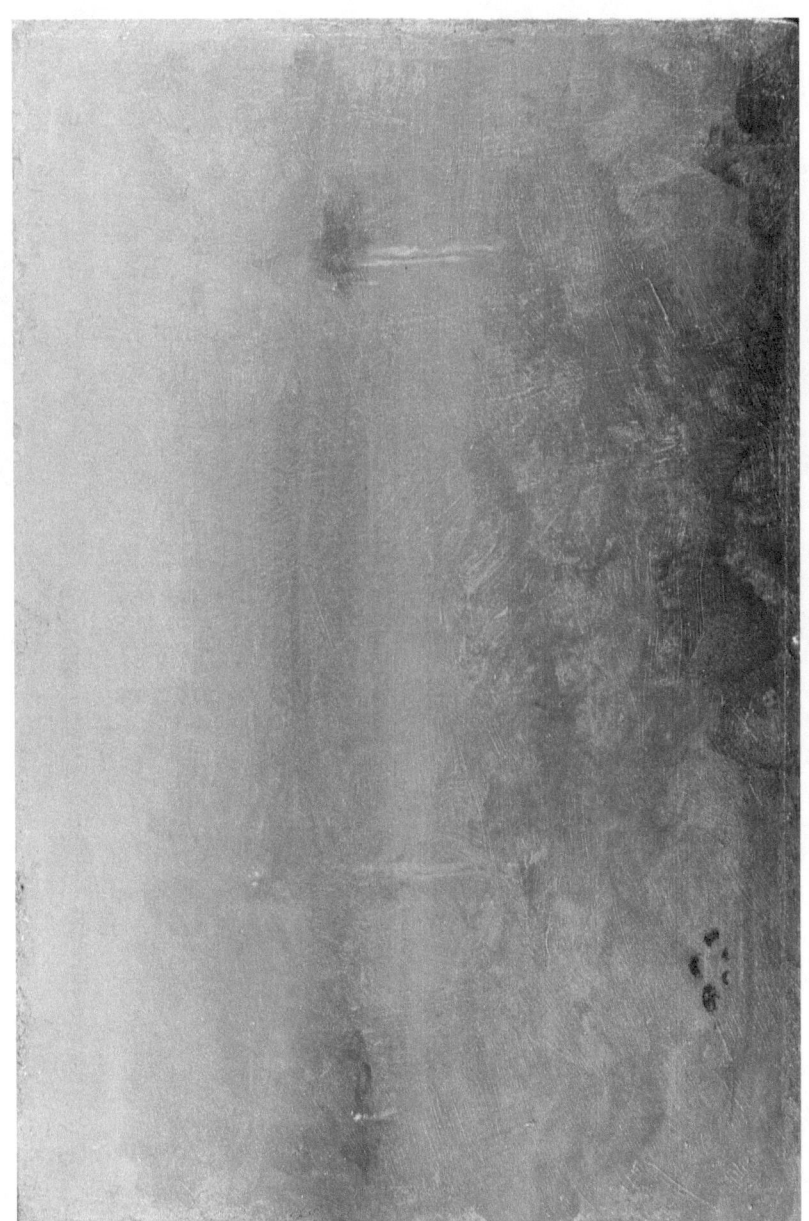

Figure 2. James McNeill Whistler, Nocturne: Silver and Opal—Chelsea (early 1880s).
Oil on wood panel. Freer Gallery of Art, Smithsonian Institution, Washington, DC.: Gift of Charles Lang Freer, F1902.146a-b.

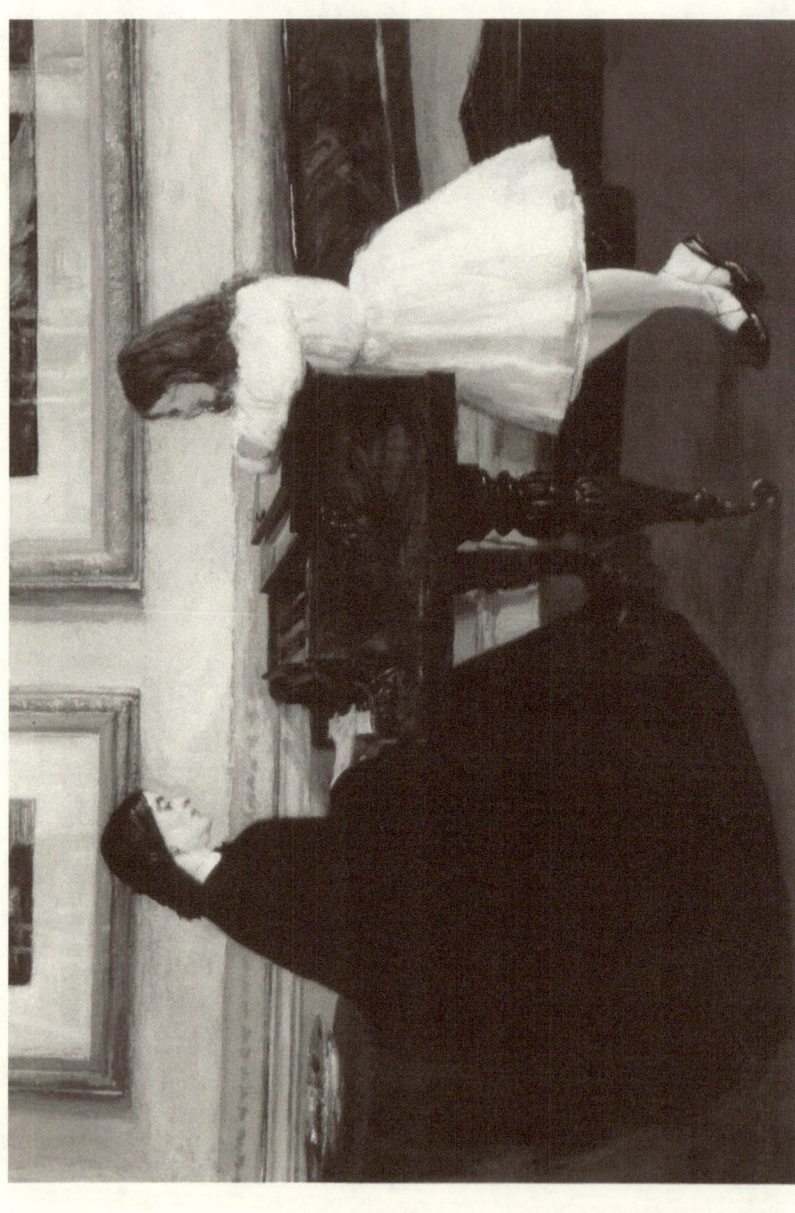

Figure 3. James McNeill Whistler, At the Piano (1858–59). Oil on canvas. Bequest of Louise Taft Semple, Taft Museum of Art, Cincinnati, OH. Courtesy of the Taft Museum of Art, Cincinnati, OH. Photo Credit: Tony Walsh, Cincinnati, OH.

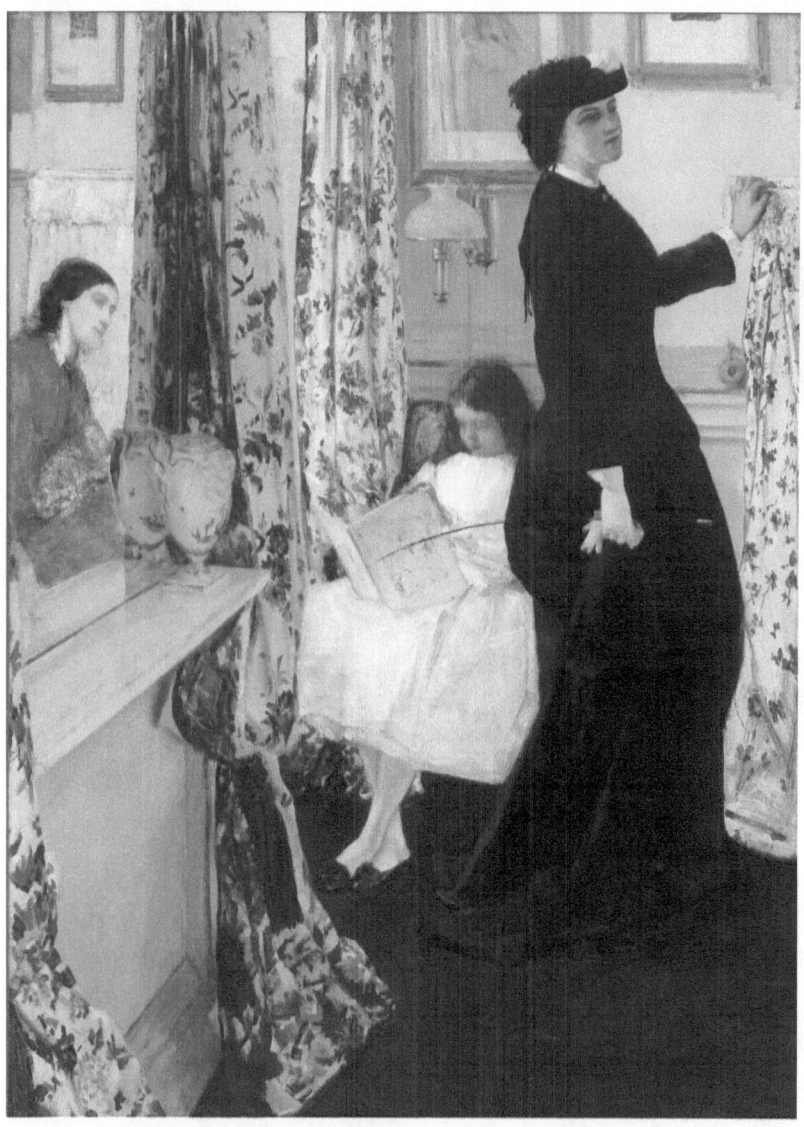

Figure 4. James McNeill Whistler, Harmony in Green and Rose: The Music Room (1860–61). Oil on canvas. Freer Gallery of Art, Smithsonian Institution, Washington, DC.: Gift of Charles Lang Freer, F1917.234a-b.

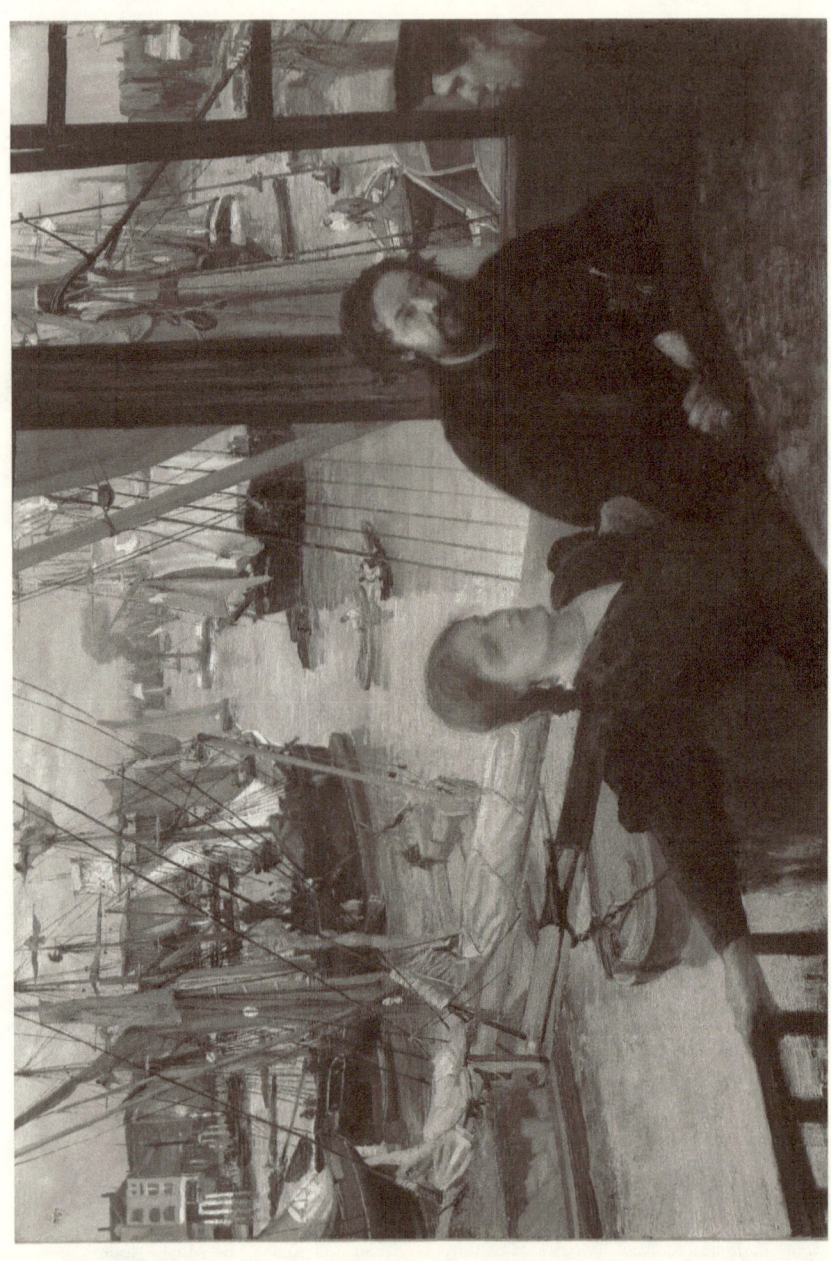

Figure 5. James McNeill Whistler, *Wapping (1860–64). Oil on canvas. John J. Whitney Collection. Image courtesy National Gallery of Art, Washington, DC.*

Hidden Lives and Unvisited Tombs

I end this study with moments from two very different novels, one an exemplary Romantic text, Goethe's *The Sorrows of Young Werther* (1774), and the other an exemplary realist text, George Eliot's *Middlemarch* (1871–72). The contrast between these works throws into relief a distinction threatened by the reductive definitions that have come to plague realism and, indeed, Romanticism, definitions that set the objectivity and comprehensiveness of realism in opposition to the emotional subjectivity of Romanticism. In the preface to *Werther*, Goethe prepares his readers for the story that is to follow. He adopts the tone of a mere editor who has collected Werther's letters; who cares deeply about the novel's subject; and who expects readers to share a uniform, predictable, emotional response to the novel:

> I have carefully collected whatever I have been able to learn of the story of poor Werther, and here present it to you, knowing that you will thank me for it. To his spirit and character you cannot refuse your admiration and love: to his fate you will not deny your tears.
>
> And thou, good soul, who sufferest the same distress as he endured once, draw comfort from his sorrows; and let this little book be thy friend, if, owing to fortune or through thine own fault, thou canst not find a dearer companion.[1]

Goethe enfolds the reader into the story by declaring the value of Werther's "spirit and character" and positioning the reader as admirer and friend. In addition to framing the reader's relationship to Werther, the preface also frames the reader's relationship to the novel. "The little book" itself can function as a friend to the reader, in moments when the reader is in need.

The novel's structure works hard to enact the relationships detailed in this preface. With its one-sided epistolary form, *The Sorrows of Young Werther* situates its reader as the recipient of Werther's letters, and Werther addresses the reader as "dear friend" in the first lines of the first letter. Further, Werther's narrative focuses almost exclusively on his interactions with others; he falls in love, he endears himself to the locals, he offends his employer, he goes mad when his love rejects him. When he believes he has lost the relationships that were most important to him, and feeling himself quite alone, Werther commits suicide. *The Sorrows of Young Werther* ends with his lonely burial, and the novel's last, stark line reads "No clergyman attended."

One hundred years later, George Eliot opens *Middlemarch* with a prelude in which she describes her heroine Dorothea Brooke in terms of what she is not: no Saint Theresa, defined by indefiniteness, "foundress of nothing." Not only is there no "coherent social faith and order" in which women such as Dorothea could locate an outlet for their yearnings and ambitions, there is no community of friends to which they belong: "a cygnet is reared uneasily among the ducklings in the brown pond, and never finds the living stream in fellowship with its own oary-footed kind."[2] The central figure is introduced not as a heroine to be admired or loved, but rather as an odd creature, out of place in her own time, and lost among a sea of others who bear no resemblance to her.

Middlemarch ends, as it begins, considering Dorothea's relation to the world and those around her:

> Her finely touched spirit had still its fine issues, though they were not widely visible. Her full nature, like that river of which Cyrus broke the strength, spent itself in channels which had no great name on the earth. But the effect of her being on those around her was incalculably diffusive: for the growing good of the world is partly dependent on unhistoric acts; and that things are not so ill with you and me as they might have been, is half owing to the number who lived faithfully a hidden life, and rest in unvisited tombs. (838)

In Eliot's construction, the "hidden life" and "unvisited tomb" are not signs of rejection, alienation, or abandonment. Rather, they are a necessary consequence of the realities of a social order that is not ideally suited to the temperament and desire of every individual. And still, in spite of or perhaps because of the mysteries that define human existence, the effect of an individual on those around her is incalculable, diffuse. Dorothea might not be a celebrated martyr, but the "growing good of the world" depends on the unknown acts of Dorothea and those like her.

For Goethe's novel presumes a universal response to its content, and it affects so thorough a portrait of an individual that merely reading his letters can serve as the basis of friendship. Eliot's novel, on the other hand, asserts from beginning to end the strangeness of Dorothea, a woman who does not even know herself fully. And so in a narrative of infinitely greater complexity and length than *The Sorrows of Young Werther*, Eliot frames *Middlemarch* by reminding readers not what they know or what they will know, but rather what they do not know and cannot know. This is the work of realism: to describe alterity through the recognition, representation, and reification of the limits of the self. The unknowable other serves to check the expansive knowledge of the external world that is the other central concern of the realist enterprise.

Indeed, the vast historical and stylistic differences between the works (and there are many) do not overwhelm the shift in conception of the relationship between the individual and the other, or between the book and the reader, evident in these novels. Goethe defines the relationship between reader and text as one of identification and admiration. We will admire and love Werther; we will feel his pain. The text that tells his story will be our companion in loneliness, itself a friend. And though no clergyman attends Werther's funeral, and though his suicide is intended to pain those who were his friends by completing a long cycle of attraction and repulsion, we readers *are* there at his burial, faithful to the end of the narrative. *Werther* thus demonstrates—perhaps unintentionally—the precarious separation between identification and empathy. If we feel all of Werther's feelings with him, if we experience his joy and his sorrow, how can we distinguish our joy or pain from his? When are we being empathic toward the radical other, and when are we simply being aware of our own feelings?

Eliot uses a prelude and finale to structure her insistence not on identification but rather on mystery, diffuseness, and the hidden. Dorothea's is a story of not fitting in; her assumptions even about herself are constantly assailed. If Dorothea can't know herself, could the book claim to know her? Could its readers? Eliot escapes from this potential bind by foregrounding the lack of knowledge and uncertainty of situation that defines Dorothea's life. Eliot places that uncertainty at the center of the novel, and what results is a generous vision of the unknown and unremarkable. The beauty of the hidden life and unvisited tomb is precisely that we may never know exactly the greatness of the impact of those lives. And in that recognition of a true alterity exists the space for empathic extension.

The goal of this study was to establish the ways that alterity arises in realist texts and images, and to consider how depictions of unique individuals test the limits of representation. I have further attempted to work through the tension that underpins the realist project: how empathic extension can occur in light of those limitations. If we recognize that the radical alterity of the other is a feature of lived experience, it becomes clear that realists' strategies for representing the unknowability of the other do not undermine their project but rather enhance it. By emphasizing the impossibility of knowing a character purely by knowing her story, and the impossibility of regarding the novel or the painting as an other, realists break away from the literary and pictorial traditions that preceded their own. This condition of not knowing the other does not damn the individual to a life of solitude or misery, a fact that distinguishes realism from other movements that follow. Perhaps it took Levinas to articulate a vocabulary that could account for both the ethical imperative that drives the realist project and the insistence on the limitations of representation that define its aesthetics. His descriptions of intersubjectivity construct the relationship between the self and the other as one of insurmountable difference, yet he asserts that the potential for an ethical engagement with the other exists in and only in the recognition of that difference: the lesson of realism that we might come to know is that we can never fully come to know the human other. Realist works temper the starkness of radical and insurmountable alterity with the awareness that such recognition requires work, which is itself edifying. Learning to read realist novels and paintings depends on the realization that we might never know the other fully, but that as a consequence of that inherent mystery, "things are not so ill with you and me as they might have been."

NOTES

NOTES TO PREFACE

1. Wayne Booth, *The Company We Keep: An Ethics of Fiction* (Berkeley: University of California Press, 1988), 485.
2. E. M. Forster, *Aspects of the Novel* (New York: Harvest Books, 1956), 63–64.
3. Ibid., 63.

INTRODUCTION

1. Charles Dickens, *David Copperfield* (London: Penguin, 2004), 356–57.
2. Attributed to Ruskin in "Review of *Perspective: Its Principle and Practice*," *The Art-Journal* 7 (1 June 1850): 202; also cited in Donald Stone, "Beauty Running in the World," *Sewanee Review* 107, no. 4 (Fall 1999): 618–25; and H. Cliff Morgan, "The Schools of the Royal Academy," *British Journal of Educational Studies* 21, no. 1 (February 1973): 94.
3. John Ruskin, "The Fighting Téméraire Tugged to Her Last Berth to Be Broken Up (1838)," in *Great Pictures as Seen and Described by Famous Writers*, ed. Esther Singleton (London: Dodd, Mead and Co., 1899), 306–8.
4. Dana Huntley, "Greatest Painting in Britain," *British Heritage* 26, no. 6 (January 2006): 8.
5. Ezra Pound, "Ezra Pound on Turner, 1909," *Tate Britain: Turner Online*, http://www.tate.org.uk/britain/turner/pound.htm.
6. Erich Auerbach, *Mimesis* (Princeton, NJ: Princeton University Press, 1953), 515.
7. See Peter Brooks's *Realist Visions* for a thorough analysis of these intersections (New Haven, CT: Yale University Press, 2005).
8. Franco Moretti in "Serious Century" and Garrett Stewart in *The Look of Reading* offer cogent and insightful analyses of paintings while nevertheless perpetuating this tendency. I hope to avoid this tendency by considering Whistler's paintings in light of his condemnation of such will-to-narrate. "Serious Century," in *History, Geography, and Culture*, vol. 1 of *The Novel*, ed. Franco Moretti (Princeton, NJ: Princeton University Press, 2006), 364–400. *The Look of Reading: Book, Painting,*

and Text (Chicago: University of Chicago Press, 2006).

9. Pliny, Chapter 36, Book XXXV, from *Natural History* (London: Bell and Sons, 1898), 249–51.

10. Cf. Norman Bryson, *Vision and Painting: The Logic of the Gaze* (New Haven, CT: Yale University Press, 1983).

11. Later, surrealists would playfully reject this boundary: Magritte's *La trahison des images* (1929) is an excellent example, with its *"ceci n'est pas une pipe"* written beneath the image of a pipe.

12. Oscar Wilde, *The Picture of Dorian Gray* (New York: Norton, 1988), 3.

13. Think of George Eliot's anticipating readerly reaction in the seventeenth chapter of *Adam Bede*.

14. "Is Literary Theory a Science?" in *Realism and Representation: Essays on the Problem of Realism in Relation to Science, Literature, and Culture*, ed. George Levine (Madison: University of Wisconsin Press, 1993), 155.

15. Bernard Weinberg, *French Realism: The Critical Reaction, 1830–1870* (London: Oxford University Press, 1937).

16. Levine, "Looking for the Real," introduction to *Realism and Representation*, 9–10.

17. Michael Boyd, *The Reflexive Novel* (Lewisburg, PA: Bucknell University Press, 1983), 18. Boyd argues that the "reflexive" novels of Joyce, Woolf, Nabokov, and others are "anti-realist." He thus cannot allow that the realist writer was similarly reflexive, and that the reflection was in fact constitutive of realism itself.

18. D. A. Williams, ed., *The Monster in the Mirror* (London: Oxford University Press, 1978), 257–58.

19. Honoré de Balzac, *La Peau du chagrin*, in *Oeuvres complètes* (Paris: Editions de Delta, 1976), 558.

20. George Eliot, *Adam Bede* (London: Penguin, 2008), 177.

21. *Le Salut Public*, March 26, 1865: " . . . il ne saurait reproduire ce qui est dans sa réalité: il n'a apercu les objects qu'au travers de son proper temperament." Cited in David Bellos, *Balzac Criticism in France 1850–1900* (London: Clarendon Press, 1976), 99.

22. Charles Dickens, *Oliver Twist* (London: Penguin, 1985), 34. Later in the preface, Dickens concludes about his novel that "It is true"; written in all caps, it echoes Balzac's claim in *Le Père Goriot* that "All is true."

23. Lilian R. Furst, *All Is True: The Claims and Strategies of Realist Fiction* (Durham, NC: Duke University Press, 1995), 9.

24. A few years after Zola's works were first translated into English and published, a "National Vigilance Association" was formed to quell the spread of "pernicious literature," and Zola's publisher, Henry Vizetelly, was tried for selling obscenity. Ernest Vizetelly, *Émile Zola, Novelist and Reformer* (London: J. Lane, 1904), 242–99.

25. England was not alone in its outrage at Zola's novels: many in his own country (Brunetiere included) concurred with British assessments, and German critics (for example) responded in kind: Naturalism was called "pig literature [Ferkel-literatur]," in the German press, and Zola's novels in particular ignited the following sentiments: "it is impossible to read a single page of [*L'Assommoir*] aloud before respectable people"; "one does not know how to take up this work critically without dirtying his fingers"; "the author wallows, and the reader with

him, in the vilest muck"; and *"La Joie de vivre* is an olla-porrida of blood, mucus, and stomach secretions." Such reactions, from wherever they arose, did little to discourage the public from reading the novels, as Zola's sales naturally increased as a consequence of the court's attention. Winthrop Hegeman Root, *German Criticism of Zola, 1875–1893* (New York: Columbia University Press, 1931), 7.

26. See also Lawrence Schehr in *Figures of Alterity: French Realism and Its Others*: "Since the text is that which is woven and unwoven [. . .], realism would be that which most clearly shows the incompatibility of the real (or even the Real, in the Lacanian sense) with the literary. Narrative can inscribe the absence of the real, so that anything that rewrites this act of inscription is rewriting the primary gestures of literature" (Palo Alto, CA: Stanford University Press, 2003), 7.

27. From the 1859 first edition. George Eliot, *Adam Bede*, 630, n1.

28. Amanda Anderson, *The Powers of Distance: Cosmopolitanism and the Cultivation of Detachment* (Princeton, NJ: Princeton University Press, 2001).

29. Ibid., 6.

30. Ibid., 6 (author's italics). Cf. Levine: "Perhaps in part because of this kind of danger, Evelyn Keller has sought to preserve an idea of objectivity as 'the pursuit of a maximally authentic, and hence maximally reliable, understanding of the world around oneself.'" "Looking for the Real," 11.

31. George Eliot, "The Natural History of German Life," in *Selected Essays, Poems, and Other Writings* (London: Penguin, 1990), 107–39.

32. Tim Barringer, "Images of Otherness and the Visual Production of Difference: Race and Labour in Illustrated Texts, 1850–1865," in *The Victorians and Race*, ed. Shearer West (Brookfield, VT: Ashgate Press, 1996), 34.

33. Ibid., 35.

34. Eliot's resistance to wholesale detachment brings into focus perhaps the most investigated alterity of Victorian fiction: the colonized other, whose very difference amplifies or defines the Britishness of the novelist or a novel's characters. Obviously, studies on Victorian engagement with colonization are myriad. If, as Regenia Gagnier writes, "the masked Other" functions "as the self, building itself through opposition to Others and undoing itself in the isolation of its own hard-bounded ego," then the relationship between the British and the colonized exists outside of the radical alterity required of interpersonal relationships. "Review of *Rule of Darkness: British Literature and Imperialism, 1830–1914* by Patrick Brantlinger," *Modern Philology* 87, no. 3 (February 1990): 316. Those relationships to the physically distant stranger are based not on a real apprehension of distinctive and individual alterity but on a wholesale dialectic that inhibits an ethical relationship. Focusing on the Realists' relationship with the colonized in relation to Eliot's nuanced formulations of representation allows Nancy Henry, for example, to explore "a disjunction between the expressed politics of a realist aesthetic that did not permit Eliot to represent what she had not seen, and life in a society that encouraged practical decisions based on abstractions—the colonies." *George Eliot and the British Empire* (Cambridge: Cambridge University Press, 2000), 9. While not dismissing this important work, I must note that my interest is in another kind of relationship depicted in these works—not with those whom characters assume *are* the wholesale other, but with those whom characters do not accord alterity.

35. Kay Young, *"Middlemarch* and the Problem of Other Minds Heard," *Literature, Interpretation, Theory* 14 (2003): 230.

36. John Stuart Mill, *On Liberty and other Essays*, ed. John Gray (Oxford: Oxford University Press, 1991), 42–43. Also cited in Anderson's *Detachment*, 17.

37. George Levine, *Dying to Know: Scientific Epistemology and Narrative in Victorian England* (Chicago: University of Chicago Press, 2002), 269.

38. Ibid., 271.

39. "As I conceive it, this moral perfectionism is a particular narrative form (rather than a concept, theory, or disposition) capable of great variation and extension. At its heart is the complex proposition that we turn from our ordinary lives, realize an ideal self, and perfect what is distinctly human in us—and that we do so in response to exemplary others. How exactly do we become better? Certainly we often imagine ourselves improving through following rules, commandments, laws, guidelines. Without denying this, moral perfectionism stresses another means of improvement, one in which individual transfiguration comes not through obedience to such codes but through openness to example—through responsive, unpredictable engagements with other people." Miller is careful to note that this movement-toward lacks finitude, writing that "it bears repeating that none of these mechanisms has the power to banish skepticism in any final or conclusive fashion." Andrew Miller, *The Burdens of Perfection: On Ethics and Reading in Nineteenth-Century British Literature* (Ithaca, NY: Cornell University Press, 2008), 4, 25.

40. Ibid., 272.

41. I do not claim to offer a comprehensive overview of notions of sympathy and empathy as understood from the eighteenth through the nineteenth centuries, as others have done that work far more effectively than I can here. See David Marshall's *The Surprising Effects of Sympathy* (Chicago: University of Chicago Press, 1988), Rachel Ablow's *The Marriage of Minds: Reading Sympathy in the Victorian Marriage Plot* (Stanford, CA: Stanford University Press, 2007), and Suzanne Keen's *Empathy and the Novel* (Princeton, NJ: Princeton University Press, 2007), for clear overviews of the tradition.

42. Audrey Jaffe, *Scenes of Sympathy: Identity and Representation in Victorian Fiction* (Ithaca, NY: Cornell University Press, 2000), 8.

43. Ibid., 15.

44. David Marshall, *The Surprising Effects of Sympathy*, 1. Ethical literary criticism arises from the knowledge that readers do attempt to enter into the sentiments of characters within fiction. Wayne Booth's description of the ethics of fiction is even less invasive, as one need not "enter into" a character's sentiments but can learn from a character's actions, the text itself serving as a "relatively cost-free offer of trial runs." *The Company We Keep: An Ethics of Fiction* (Berkeley: University of California Press, 1988), 485. As Jil Larson notes, the recuperation of ethical criticism begun by Booth and Martha Nussbaum sought to avoid the essentializing tendency of reductive moralizing without completely excluding ethics from literary analysis. Larson follows in their path, and her work along with the work of others reinvigorating ethical criticism paved the way for studies such as this one. *Ethics and Narrative in the English Novel, 1880–1914* (Cambridge: Cambridge University Press, 2001).

45. David Hume, *A Treatise of Human Nature* (London: John Noon, 1886), 365.

46. Adam Smith, *The Theory of Moral Sentiment* (London: Henry G. Bohn, 1853), 3.

47. Ibid., 4.

48. Marshall, *The Surprising Effects of Sympathy*, 3.

49. Catherine Gallagher, *Nobody's Story: The Vanishing Acts of Women Writers in the Marketplace 1670–1820* (Berkeley: University of California Press, 1995), 170.

50. Ibid., 168.

51. Ibid., 169.

52. Suzanne Keen, *Empathy and the Novel*, xii.

53. Rachel Ablow, *The Marriage of Minds*, 6.

54. Letter, July 5, 1859; author's italics. John Cross, vol. 2 of *George Eliot's Life as Related in Her Letters and Journals* (London: Blackwell and Sons, 1885), 118.

55. Paul Cobley, *Narrative* (London: Routledge, 2001), 92–93.

56. Felicia Bonaparte, *Will and Destiny: Morality and Tragedy in George Eliot's Novels* (New York: New York University Press, 1975), 163, 169. Ellen Argyros, also writing about sympathy in Eliot's works, produces a similar conclusion about the sympathy engendered by Eliot's novels: sympathy is "a kind of imaginative transportation beyond the boundaries of the self and its most egoistic claims to a recognition of the differences between self and other." *"Without Any Check of Proud Reserve": Sympathy and Its Limits in George Eliot's Novels* (New York: Peter Lang, 1999), 1.

57. George Eliot, *Middlemarch* (London: Penguin Books, 1994), 643.

58. Honoré de Balzac, *Le Père Goriot* (Paris: Pocket Books, 1989), 33. "Il s'y rencontrera toujours un lieu vierge, un antre inconnu, des fleurs, des perles, des monstres, quelque chose d'inouï, oublié par les plongeurs littéraires."

59. Tobin Siebers, *Morals and Stories* (New York: Columbia University Press, 1992), 203; Roland Barthes, "The Man-Eater," in *Critical Essays on Émile Zola*, ed. David Baguley (Boston: G. K. Hall and Co., 1955), 93.

60. *Time and the Other*, trans. Richard A. Cohen (Pittsburgh, PA: Duquesne University Press, 1987), 75.

61. "The Proximity of the Other," in *Is It Righteous to Be? Interviews with Emmanuel Lévinas*, ed. Jill Robbins (Palo Alto, CA: Stanford University Press, 2001).

62. "The Other in Proust," in *The Levinas Reader*, ed. Seán Hand (London: Blackwell, 1989), 160–65; 163.

63. Ibid., 164–65.

64. James R. Mensch, *Hiddenness and Alterity: Philosophical and Literary Sightings of the Unseen* (Pittsburgh, PA: Duquesne University Press, 2005), 3.

65. "[. . .] labor in its possessive grasp suspends the independence of the element: its being. The thing evinces this hold or this comprehension—this ontology. Possession neutralizes this being: as property the thing is an existent that has lost its being. [. . .] Possession masters, suspends, postpones the unforeseeable future of the element—its independence, its being [. . .] Labor in its primary intention is this acquisition, this movement toward oneself; it is not a transcendence." Levinas, *Totality and Infinity: An Essay on Exteriority* (Pittsburgh, PA: Duquesne University Press, 1969), 158–59.

66. David P. Haney, "Aesthetics and Ethics in Gadamer, Levinas, and Romanticism: Problems of Phronesis and Teche," *PMLA* 114, no. 1 (January 1999): 43.

67. "the structure of the reader's interpretative relationship to a literary text has affinities with a person's ethical relationship to others." Ibid., 38.

68. Ibid., 40.

69. Adam Zachary Newton, *Narrative Ethics* (Cambridge, MA: Harvard Univer-

sity Press, 1995), 13. Newton goes on to make the parallel between the story and the person explicit: "Stories, like persons, originate alogically. As ethical performance, in Levinas' sense, they are concussive; they shock and linger as 'traumatisms of astonishment.'" Ibid., 13.

70. In *What Do Pictures Want?* Mitchell wrestles with "the peculiar tendency of images to absorb and be absorbed by human subjects in processes that look suspiciously like those of living things," regarding that tendency not a problem that must be shut down by criticism, but rather a valuable mode of experiencing images. *What Do Pictures Want? The Lives and Loves of Images* (Chicago: University of Chicago Press, 2005), 2.

71. Dorothy Hale, *Social Formalism: The Novel in Theory from Henry James to the Present* (Stanford, CA: Stanford University Press, 1998), 8.

72. Levinas, "Reality and Its Shadow," in *The Levinas Reader,* 139.

73. Levinas, *Otherwise than Being* (Pittsburgh, PA: Duquesne University Press, 1969), 183.

CHAPTER ONE

1. Rosemarie Bodenheimer, *Knowing Dickens* (Ithaca, NY: Cornell University Press, 2007), 17.

2. John Forster, *The Life of Charles Dickens* (London: Lippincott and Co., 1874), 47–70.

3. Bodenheimer argues that these moments are typical of Dickens's anxiety to convince the reader who might not otherwise believe him, a hyperexertion of truth, but one that is overdetermined by his desire.

4. Forster, 23, 24, 27.

5. Charles Dickens, *Great Expectations* (London: Penguin, 2002), 248. Subsequent citations of *Great Expectations* will be given parenthetically in text.

6. These failures are nevertheless constructive and instructive. John Fenstermaker addresses the often overlooked role of the failure of language in *Bleak House:* "The central symptom of much of the sickness Dickens examines is the failure of words, written and spoken, to express truth and to communicate genuine human fellow-feeling. Too often language is used, as the narrator says, 'under false pretences of all sorts' to effect 'trickery, evasion, procrastination, spoliation [and] botheration,' creating 'influences that can never come to good.'" "Language Abuse in *Bleak House:* The First Monthly Installment," in *Victorian Literature and Society,* ed. James Kincaid (Columbus: The Ohio State University Press, 1984), 241.

7. Charles Dickens, *A Tale of Two Cities* (London: Penguin, 2003), 14. Subsequent citations of *A Tale of Two Cities* will be given parenthetically in text.

8. Robert Alter, "The Demons of History in Dickens' *Tale,*" *NOVEL: A Forum on Fiction* 2, no. 2 (Winter 1969): 139.

9. Barbara Lecker, "The Split Characters of Charles Dickens," *Studies in English Literature, 1500–1900* 19, no. 4 (Autumn 1979): 698. Later, Lecker argues, Dickens will unite the heart and head in single characters, such as the "happily schizoid" Wemmick in *Great Expectations.* Ibid., 699.

10. Some examples: "don't heed me any more than if I was a speaking machine" (25); "I am a mere machine" (25); and, as repeated several times, "I am a man of business" (25, 83, 101, 151, 210, 212). Its fullest iteration is uttered at the peak of the

Parisian drama, when Lorry is in danger of losing the only family he has known: "I have been a man of business, ever since I have been a man. Indeed, I may say that I was a man of business when a boy" (322).

11. A critique that applies regardless of the class of the perpetrator. Foulon's dismissive "let them eat grass" is matched by the brutality of the mob's attack and decapitation of Foulon.

12. Estella refers to Miss Havisham as her "mother by adoption" (304). See also Hilary Schor, *Dickens and the Daughter of the House* (Cambridge: Cambridge University Press, 1999), 167.

13. Cf. Max Byrd, "Reading in *Great Expectations*," *PMLA* 91, no. 2 (1976): 259–65.

14. The resonance between this statement and Eliot's description of learning to read is impressive; see my discussion in chapter 2.

15. Monique Morgan contrasts this scene of misinterpretation with Pip's last interaction with Magwitch, at the convict's death. There, she argues, physical intimacy trumps written declarations, and Pip is able to understand Magwitch through just a squeeze of his hand. "Conviction in Writing: Crime, Confession, and the Written Word in *Great Expectations*," *Dickens Study Annual* 33 (2003): 87–108.

16. Peter Brooks, *Reading for the Plot: Design and Intention in Narrative* (Cambridge, MA: Harvard University Press, 1992), 131.

17. Adam Smith, *The Theory of Moral Sentiment* (London: Henry G. Bohn, 1853), 3.

18. See, for example, Q. D. Leavis's "How We Must Read *Great Expectations*," in *Dickens the Novelist* (London: Pantheon, 1970).

19. J. Hillis Miller, *Victorian Subjects* (Durham, NC: Duke University Press, 1991), 179.

20. For example, handwriting serves to identify Dedlock's former lover and Esther's father. Here the issue is being able to discern the familiar shapes that identify an individual; the words written are, for this enterprise, meaningless. Much as Pip attempted to make out his parents in the shapes of the letters on their tombstone, character and personhood can be interpreted from the literalization of the writing.

21. David Cowles, "Methods of Inquiry, Modes of Evidence: Perception, Self-Deception, and Truth in *Bleak House*," *The Dickensian* 87, no. 425 (Autumn 1991): 159, 154. The sentiment is echoed by Camilla Humphreys, who catalogues a similar trajectory in the personal letters that populate the novel. Whereas "Court of Chancery writings confuse and obfuscate," creating "obstacles to understanding and solution," personal letters are "clear and concise and written from the heart," providing "consistent movement towards a coherence and connection." Camilla Humphreys, "Dickens's Use of Letters in *Bleak House*," *Dickens Quarterly* 6, no. 2 (June 1989): 53.

22. Graham Hough, "Language and Reality in *Bleak House*," in *Realism in European Literature*, ed. Nicholas Boyle and Martin Swales (Cambridge: Cambridge University Press, 1986), 59. Hough also echoes the formulations of Cowles and Humphreys cited above, noting that Dickens's appeal in Esther's narration is "not to experience, the conventional wisdom, or the social order; it is to the wisdom of the heart." Ibid., 65.

23. The duality of the novel's narration supports these distinctions, alternating as it does between Esther's retrospective rendering of the tale and unnamed omniscient narrative voice. The narrative oscillations help to render distinctive language patterns in a uniquely Realist way. Realism, as Graham Hough writes

with particular attention to *Bleak House,* "speaks in the language of fallible human beings who have lived too close to the events they describe for the completeness of an inventory or the precision of a diagram." Ibid., 51.

24. Harold Skimpole is another, and his aesthetic embrace of suffering and concomitant lack of action form a complement to Mrs. Jellyby. Connecting representations of such characters with altruistic action is a cornerstone of Dickens's writing and the criticism of his works. "A Christmas Carol" is perhaps his best-known work devoted (ostensibly) solely to the promotion of altruistic action in his readers by depicting characters whose primary fault is a lack of empathic action. This dynamic is undeniable in Dickens's work, but it is not my focus. Cf. Mary-Catherine Harrison's "The Paradox of Fiction and the Ethics of Empathy: Reconceiving Dickens's Realism," *Narrative* 16, no. 3 (October 2008): 256–78.

25. Charles Dickens, *Bleak House* (London: Penguin, 2003), 53. Subsequent citations of *Bleak House* will be given parenthetically in text.

26. Her problem, then, is not one of blindness, but of focus.

27. Bruce Robbins, "Telescopic Philanthropy," in *Nation and Narration,* ed. Homi K. Bhabha (New York: Routledge, 1990), 224. It is worth noting that Robbins's use of "face-to-face" is not the Levinasian formulation of the phrase.

28. "The central symptom of much of the sickness Dickens examines is the failure of words, written and spoken, to express truth and to communicate genuine human fellow-feeling." Fenstermaker, "Language Abuse in *Bleak House:* The First Monthly Installment," 241.

29. Carolyn M. Dever, "Broken Mirror, Broken Words: Autobiography, Prosopopeia and the Dead Mother in *Bleak House,*" *Studies in the Novel* 27, no. 1 (Spring 1995): 44.

30. "Among the many issues *Bleak House* explores is that of eloquence, of one person's ability by means of language to persuade another to act in the world of gesture, a world which may contain, but does not necessarily depend on, language." Sandra Young, "Uneasy Relations: Possibilities for Eloquence in *Bleak House,*" *Dickens Studies Annual* 9 (1981): 67.

31. Audrey Jaffe, *Scenes of Sympathy: Identity and Representation in Victorian Fiction* (Ithaca, NY: Cornell University Press, 2000), 29, 44.

32. Ibid., 44.

33. Paul Saint-Amour, "'Christmas Yet to Come': Hospitality, Futurity, the *Carol,* and 'The Dead,'" *Representations* 98 (Spring 2007): 99. Saint-Amour's is an argument informed by Levinasian conceptions of alterity.

34. Ibid., 99–100.

CHAPTER TWO

1. An earlier version of the *Adam Bede* analysis in this chapter appeared in "Learning to Read: Interpersonal Literacy in *Adam Bede,*" *Papers on Language and Literature* 44, no. 2 (Spring 2008): 145–67.

2. George Eliot, *Adam Bede* (London: Penguin, 2008), 215. Subsequent citations of *Adam Bede* will be given parenthetically in text.

3. In *Adam Bede,* Eliot writes, "Nature has her language, and she is not unveracious; but we don't know all the intricacies of her syntax just yet, and in a hasty reading we may happen to extract the very opposite of her real meaning." Ibid., 168.

4. July 5, 1859. John Walter Cross, *George Eliot's Life as Related in Her Letters and Journals* (London: Blackwood, 1885), 118.

5. J. Hillis Miller, *Others* (Princeton, NJ: Princeton University Press, 2001), 68.

6. Ernst Gombrich's discussion of geographical and zoological woodcuts in *Art and Illusion* offers an interesting illustration of the same tendency (London: Phaidon, 1977).

7. "The Natural History of German Life," in *Selected Essays, Poems, and Other Writings* (London: Penguin, 1990), 108–9.

8. George Eliot, *Middlemarch* (London: Penguin, 1994), 77. Subsequent citations of *Middlemarch* will be given parenthetically in text.

9. " . . . her mind had glanced over the possibility, which she would have preferred, of finding that her home would be in a parish which had a larger share of the world's misery, so that she might have had more active duties in it." Ibid., 78. Perhaps equally problematic is the fact that she accepts the curate's description as accurate.

10. Mathilde Blind, *George Eliot* (London: W. H. Allen and Co., 1883), 120, 119, 120.

11. Judith Mitchell, "George Eliot and the Problematic of Female Beauty," *Modern Language Studies* 20, no. 3 (Summer 1990): 17.

12. Ibid., 19.

13. Critical assessments have begun to unseat Eliot's heroines from these binaries. Nina Auerbach's analysis of Hetty as a "fallen woman" hinted that Hetty and Dinah have more in common than is evident at first glance. "The Rise of the Fallen Woman," *Nineteenth-Century Fiction* 35, no. 1 (January 1980): 29–53. Marina van Zuylan's later *Monomania* breaks new ground by arguing that Dorothea, a pious heroine like many others in Eliot's fiction, is the monomaniac of interest in *Middlemarch* (not Casaubon with his *Key to All Mythologies*), as her commitment to the purely altruistic bettering of others' lives compels her disavowal of her own desire, and indeed her own physicality. Van Zuylan's argument thus removes Dorothea from the seat of piety and in turn considers her as more fully human by noting the limitations of her self-understanding. *Monomania* (Ithaca, NY: Cornell University Press, 2005). Caroline Levine similarly complicates our understanding of Dinah through her analysis of visual alterity in *Adam Bede;* she views Dinah and Hetty as contrasting examples used by Eliot to communicate a message of ethical viewing, concluding that Eliot endorses a normative heterosexuality through the novel's repudiation of Hetty's actions. *The Serious Pleasures of Suspense: Victorian Realism and Narrative Doubt* (Charlottesville: University of Virginia Press, 2003). I propose a further reconsideration of Dinah and Hetty by exploring not their differences (well-established both within the novel and in its criticism) but rather the similarities of their parallel journeys though the text by focusing not only on the way women see others or see themselves but also on the way they control others' readings of their bodies. Eliot provides a useful paradigm for this consideration through the act of reading as defined in "Book Second" and throughout *Adam Bede:* learning to read offers a means of achieving humanity for the characters within the novel. See also Jennifer Uglow's *George Eliot* (London: Virago, 1987) and Alan Bellringer's *George Eliot* (New York: St. Martin's, 1993). More current forays into Hetty's plight include Neil Hertz's *George Eliot's Pulse* (Palo Alto, CA: Stanford University Press: 2003), Bernard Paris's *Rereading George Eliot: Changing Responses to Her Experiments in Life* (Albany: State University of New York Press, 2003), and

Nancy Marck's "Narrative Transference and Female Narcissism: The Social Message of *Adam Bede*," *Studies in the Novel* 35, no. 4 (Winter 2003): 447–69.

14. This explication is buttressed by Eliot's inclusion of the language of phrenology and physiognomy in the text, which is documented in N. N. Feltes's "Phrenology: From Lewes to George Eliot," *Studies in the Literary Imagination* 1, no. 1 (April 1968): 13–22, and in T. R. Wright's "From Bumps to Morals: The Phrenological Background to George Eliot's Moral Framework," *The Review of English Studies* 33, no. 129 (February 1982): 34–46.

15. George Willis Cooke, *George Eliot: A Critical Study of Her Life, Writings and Philosophy* (Boston: J. Osgood, 1884), 267.

16. In chapter 3, I discuss a related dynamic in Thomas Hardy's *Tess of the d'Urbervilles*, where Tess's similar complicity highlights the distinction between the individual and the narrative of her life.

17. This inability is mutual, as demonstrated by the marked use of animal or nonhuman metaphors to describe Hetty: her ears are like shells, her cheeks like rose petals, and her lashes like flower stamens (even the narrator describes her not as a girl, but as a "dear young, round, soft, flexible *thing*"). She is compared to a kitten no fewer than seven times through the novel, calling to mind not only the precocious cuteness of the animal but also its sharp claws: "It is a beauty like that of kittens" (92); "kitten-like maiden" (92); "this kitten-like Hetty" (403); "She was like a kitten, and had the same distractingly pretty looks" (228); "she put up her round cheek against his, like a kitten" (390); "kitten-like glances" (167); "as if he had seen a kitten setting up its back" (286).

18. Peter Brooks, *Realist Vision* (New Haven, CT: Yale University Press, 2005), 99.

19. Hetty's most famous instance of being late is when, prior to marrying Adam, "she had waited and waited, in the blind vague hope that something would happen to set her free from her terror; but she could wait no longer" (396). Hetty is late; or rather, her period is late, as she is pregnant.

20. Stephen Gill, Introduction to *Adam Bede*, by George Eliot (London: Penguin, 1980), xxx.

21. Barbara Hardy, *Rituals: Feelings in the Novels of George Eliot* (London: University of Swansea Press, 1973), 7.

22. In this respect, my reading diverges from Miller's in *Others*. While much of this chapter, and indeed much of this book, owes a debt to Miller's unique analysis of alterities in Eliot's (and others') fiction, I want very much to suggest that the novel—through the narrator—insists on its own limits. Miller, on the other hand, sees a tension between the limitations of the characters and the omniscience of the narrator: "[. . .] the narrator of *Middlemarch* has precisely a 'keen vision and feeling of all ordinary human life' and can deploy such vision at will. The narrator has the same kind of keen vision that destroys the protagonist of 'The Lifted Veil.' It is just such vision that the narrator of *Middlemarch* [. . .] says we are lucky not to have." *Others*, 75.

23. Before she can love Adam and accept his proposal, Dinah must move into a space that is uncomfortable for her and that she has tried to avoid—a space where her conscious and psychical desire cannot be repressed. I discuss that movement more fully in "Learning to Read: Interpersonal Literacy in *Adam Bede*."

24. In Marina van Zuylan's characterization, Dorothea is intent on dulling the banality of a woman's existence in rural England with an active devotion to causes that demand her selflessness. Via this active refutation of her self, the argument

goes, Dorothea manages to gain the very control that she is denied in most arenas of her life. *Monomania,* 99–119.

25. A typical example, from Sidney Colvin's January 1873 review in the *Fortnightly Review:* "For the general lesson of the book, it is not easy to feel quite sure what it is, or how much importance the author gives it. In her prelude and conclusion both, she seems to insist upon the design of illustrating the necessary disappointment of a woman's nobler aspirations in a society not made to second noble aspirations in a woman. And that is one of the most burning lessons which any author could set themselves to illustrate." Cited in David Carroll, ed., *George Eliot: The Critical Heritage* (New York: Barnes and Noble, 1971), 337.

26. The *OED* cites first figurative usage dating from 1874, relatively contemporary with the writing of *Middlemarch.*

27. This is, of course, Emmanuel Levinas's formulation.

28. Here Eliot's difference from Dickens is clear, as in his novels a character's insistence on his or her own difference from the crowd or the usual *is* often enough to ensure empathic extension.

29. *The Lifted Veil* easily deserves extended analysis. Given that such analysis has been performed by Thomas Albrecht in his article "Sympathy and Telepathy: The Problems of Ethics in George Eliot's *The Lifted Veil,*" it is not worth revisiting ground he has covered so well. My primary dissent from his argument, which otherwise directly anticipates my critical approach, is that he does not go far enough in addressing the significance of Latimer's relationship with the unknown. *ELH* 73, no. 2 (2006): 437–63.

30. Sally Shuttleworth, Introduction to *The Lifted Veil and Brother Jacob,* by George Eliot (London: Penguin, 2001), xiii.

31. Eliot, *The Lifted Veil,* 15.

32. Kate Flint, "Blood, Bodies, and *The Lifted Veil,*" *Nineteenth-Century Literature* 51, no. 4 (March 1997): 456.

33. Ibid., 472.

34. Cf. Albrecht, "Sympathy and Telepathy."

35. Rae Greiner's article on *The Lifted Veil* was published just weeks before this study was completed. In it, she gestures toward the idea that Albrecht articulates and that is the central focus of this study: empathic extension was not necessarily predicated on identification. She traces Eliot's depiction of that idea to Adam Smith, emphasizing the narrative time in which sympathetic extension is always situated. She does not, however, go so far as to say that the other cannot be known, only that the movement into knowledge takes time and that Eliot acknowledges its limitation with regard to the reader: "Eliot had reservations about the degree to which such intimacy with others' thought prompted ethical responses in us." "Sympathy Time: Adam Smith, George Eliot, and the Realist Novel," *Narrative* 17, no. 3 (October 2009): 306.

CHAPTER THREE

1. Desmond Hawkins, *Thomas Hardy* (London: A. Barker, 1950), 17. Kathleen Blake articulates Sue's character beautifully, and cites Hawkins's comment, in "Sue Bridehead, 'Woman of the Feminist Movement,'" *Studies in English Literature* 18, no. 4 (Autumn 1978): 703–26.

2. Hardy writes to Florence Henniker on August 12, 1895, "Curiously enough, I am more interested in the Sue story than in any I have written," in *Collected Letters of Thomas Hardy*, vol. 2, *1893–1901*, ed. Richard Little Purdy and Michael Millgate (London: Clarendon Press, 1980). See also Elizabeth Langland's "A Perspective of One's Own: Thomas Hardy and the Elusive Sue Bridehead," *Studies in the Novel* 12, no. 1 (Spring 1980): 14; and Maria DiBattista's *First Love: The Affections of Modern Fiction* (Chicago: University of Chicago Press, 1991), 94.

3. This is of course Brooks's thesis in *Reading for the Plot:* "the absolutism of the desire from which narrative as narrating is born: it is in essence the desire to be heard, recognized, understood, which, never wholly satisfied or indeed satisfiable, continues to generate the desire to tell, the effort to enunciate a significant version of the life story in order to captivate a possible listener" (54); "desire comes into being as a perpetual want for (of) a satisfaction the cannot be offered in reality" (55) (Cambridge, MA: Harvard University Press, 1992).

4. Langland, "A Perspective of One's Own," 12.

5. "That Sue is enmeshed in Jude's limited point of view, then, helps account for our sense of inconsistencies in her character. We attempt to judge as a personality in her own right a figure intended to serve merely to define another personality. Often, when Jude looks at his cousin, he in fact gazes into a mirror which reflects the image of his own ambivalence" (ibid., 15). "Most critics have seen Sue's inconsistency in this sway. But as we have seen, the consequences of this perspective are a sense that the grinder of analysis is an inadequate tool for capturing Sue's characters. A more radical inconsistency emerges when the character is inconsistent with her own personality; that is, the creator has failed to create a completely credible individual, or the creator finds those adhesive tapes of shopworn philosophy—this time about women—easier to apply than to reexamine the premise of his narrative framework" (ibid., 17–18). Sue is not the only focus of attempts to erase ambiguity from Hardy's heroines. W. Eugene Davis tries his best to sort out plot gaps that would explain Tess's purity or lack thereof in *"Tess of the d'Urbervilles:* Some Ambiguities about a Pure Woman," *Nineteenth-Century Fiction* 22, no. 4 (March 1968): 397–401.

6. Thomas Hardy, *Jude the Obscure* (London: Penguin, 1998), 136, 137. Subsequent citations of *Jude the Obscure* will be given parenthetically in text.

7. John Kucich, *The Power of Lies: Transgression in Victorian Literature* (Ithaca, NY: Cornell University Press, 1994), 230.

8. The critical searching for stability thus mirrors the analogous seeking among the characters within the texts.

9. "Although one would think the past would be more stable and determinate than an uncertain future, in Hardy's fiction it is as subject to change, chance, and unpredictability as anything else," writes Jil Larson. *Ethics and Narrative in the English Novel, 1880–1914* (Cambridge: Cambridge University Press, 2001), 71.

10. Barbara Hardy, "Towards a Poetics of Fiction: 3) An Approach through Narrative," *Novel: A Forum on Fiction* 2, no. 1 (Autumn 1968): 11.

11. Hardy's works also call forth this distinction through their pictorial appeal. Hardy was trained as an architect before he became a writer, and his attention to visuality further situates his work in the pictorial traditions that eschew narrative moralizing; that is, his interplay with visuality aligns his work with the Dutch genre painters or the French Realists and protoimpressionists. Ruth Bernard Yeazell describes Hardy, in contrast to George Eliot, as being "more engaged in looking at pictures than in theorizing about them," an engagement that rises to the fore in his

Under the Greenwood Tree, which Hardy subtitled "A Rural Painting of the Dutch School." It was Hardy's desire to "retreat from storytelling," Yeazell argues, that led him to the subtitle. She also notes that Hardy was "an artist who continued to sketch as well as write," which gave him "more reason than most to be conscious of the difference" between image and text. *Art of the Everyday: Dutch Painting and the Realist Novel* (Princeton, NJ: Princeton University Press, 2008), 134–35.

12. Larson, *Ethics,* 113.

13. See my introduction for a fuller exploration of this tendency. See also David Haney's "Aesthetics and Ethics in Gadamer, Levinas, and Romanticism: Problems of Phronesis and Teche," and Derek Attridge's "Innovation, Literature, Ethics: Relating to the Other," both in *PMLA* 114, no. 1 (January 1999).

14. Cf. Michael J. Franklin, "'Market-Faces' and Market Forces: [Corn-]Factors in the Moral Economy of Casterbridge," *Review of English Studies* 59 (June 2008): 426–48.

15. Thomas Hardy, *The Mayor of Casterbridge* (London: Penguin, 2003), 127. Subsequent citations of *The Mayor of Casterbridge* will be given parenthetically in text.

16. Jonathan Wike, "The World as Text in Hardy's Fiction," *Nineteenth-Century Literature* 47, no. 4 (March 1993), 459.

17. Compare with Lady Dedlock's insistence on applying the strictness of her self-evaluation to all others.

18. Thomas Hardy, *Tess of the d'Urbervilles* (London: Penguin, 1998), 14, 112, 113. Subsequent citations of *Tess* will be given parenthetically in text.

19. The "raw materials of beauty" showed "in a promising degree" in the "mobile parts" of her young countenance. Hardy, *The Mayor of Casterbridge,* 26.

20. Margaret Higonnet, Introduction to *Tess of the d'Urbervilles* (London: Penguin, 1998), xxv. Tess shares this trait with Hetty Sorrel of *Adam Bede.*

21. Cf. Tony Tanner, "Colour and Movement in Hardy's *Tess of the d'Urbervilles,*" *Critical Quarterly* 10, no. 3 (1968): 219–39; Paula Roy, "Agent or Victim: Thomas Hardy's *Tess of the d'Urbervilles,*" in *Women in Literature: Reading through the Lens of Gender,* ed. Ellen S. Silber (Westport, CT: Greenwood Publishing Group, 2003), 277–79.

22. Note the connection to Emma Bovary, who fed her romantic illusions with novels. Reading more stories does not necessarily make one more aware of human nature. On the other hand, we see Tess's desire for the stability and certainty provided by the never-changing novel, a desire she eschews in other places. We also see evidence of the desire to treat the novel as a behavior manual, offering trial runs for readers.

23. Narratorial and authorial constructions are included under this rubric as well; the novel's insistence on the limitations of what is readable in the other invariably applies to the novel itself. Silverman provides a clear overview of the argument that Tess is always and only a construction of the gaze of others, as well as a useful complication of that model. Kaja Silverman, "History, Figuration, and Female Subjectivity in *Tess of the d'Urbervilles,*" *Novel: A Forum on Fiction* 18, no. 1 (Autumn 1984): 5–28.

24. These included *A Daughter of the D'Urbervilles, The Body and Soul of Sue, Too late, Beloved!, Too Late Beloved,* and *Tess of the D'Urbervilles.* J. T. Laird, "New Light on the Evolution of *Tess of the d'Urbervilles,*" *The Review of English Studies* 31, no. 124 (November 1980): 421–22.

25. Compare Tess's anxiety about her genealogy and its permanence wrought through text with, for example, the confidence and authority conferred upon the

family lineage in Austen's *Persuasion*. In that novel, the Elliots of Kellynch Hall find their sense of self in the very permanence that Tess finds problematic.

26. Hardy implicates the reader in this ambivalence by placing his characters in circumstances that consistently test the boundaries of the story's believability. Is there a point when readers, like Angel Clare, will rebel against the events presented as a part of *Tess*'s plot? Those stretches—Angel and Tess stumbling across Stonehenge in the black of night, for example—demand of the assumed reader a generosity of vision very different from the suspension of disbelief often demanded of fiction's audience.

27. J. Hillis Miller, *Thomas Hardy, Distance and Desire* (Cambridge, MA: Harvard University Press, 1970), 23.

28. Ibid., 129.

29. Ibid., 145.

30. Ibid., 149.

31. This characterization is true in both 1892's *The Pursuit of the Well Beloved* and the later version. The "Well-Beloved" is Pierston's ideal, which manifests periodically in women of all shapes and temperaments, only then to leave, and Pierston's interest in these women coincides only with the duration of the Well-Beloved's presence. He can thus argue that he has been ultimately faithful to the Well-Beloved, and if his devotion to her various incarnations falters, it is only because the ideal flees from those incarnations. He seeks a "repetition of one person in another" on three levels: his pursuit of the Well-Beloved, his pursuit of himself externalized, and his pursuit of multiple iterations of the same woman. His assessment, or even simple apprehension, of women is predicated on a mental project of matching the qualities of the existent to the qualities of the ideal and abstract. The sculptor's seeming surprise at discovering the Well-Beloved incarnated in any individual is fleeting at best, and even he admits that these discoveries are overdetermined by his desire to find: "thus looking for the next new version of the fair figure, he did not consider at the moment, though he had done so at other times, that this presentiment of meeting her was, of all presentiments, just the sort of one to work out its own fulfillment" (219). The language Pierston uses to describe women once the Well-Beloved has abandoned them—"an empty caracase," "a corpse"—suggests that the bodies of the women are simply containers for his idea, his ideal, the Well-Beloved. The one binding feature was Pierston's ability to identify her; he was, in the final analysis, the determining factor, despite his attempts to project or exteriorize his desire. *The Pursuit of the Well-Beloved* and *The Well-Beloved* (London: Penguin, 1998).

32. Tess's own solipsism is at the heart of this projection; men are not the only arbiters of this dynamic.

33. Clare's is a tangled understanding, at times reducing her to archetypes, at times reveling in her individuality-as-he-understands-it-to-be. As Kathleen Blake puts it, "the crisis of their relationship reveals his habit of generalization when it comes to Tess and his commitment to her purity in the erotic sense *and* as being so summed up by his conception of her that she must remain pure of any particular experience worth mentioning. Seeing Tess as essence and type, Angel cannot admit the relevance of experience for her, and so he refuses to hear her confession about her past affair with Alec." In "Pure Tess: Hardy on Knowing a Woman," *Studies in English Literature: 1500–1900* 22, no. 4 (Autumn 1982): 697.

34. Richard le Gallienne and Mowbray Morris cited in R. G. Cox, *Thomas Hardy:*

The Critical Heritage (London: Routledge, 1970), 178 and 215.

35. In this sense, my reading complements Jan B. Gordon's compelling reading of Tess's relationship to her personal and familial past. In "Origins, History, and the Reconstitution of Family: Tess' Journey," Gordon suggests that the novel documents the characters' various attempts to concretize a past, "filling the voids" that arise from incomplete family histories or interrupted family trees. While that desire pervades the text, it exists always in tension with the impossibility of doing so, and—even more importantly—that desire leads only to failed relationships or, more figuratively, to death. Gordon is concerned with the influence that characters' relationships with their pasts have on those characters' present actions. What Angel Clare, in Gordon's telling, learns in the course of the novel is that "the history of man is not dead people or dead facts but the history of man's imagination." *ELH* 43, no. 3 (Autumn 1976): 366–88.

36. Whereas in George Eliot's novels, recognition of alterity can be developed through education and experience, Hardy's novels suggest that recognition depends not on education or development but instead on the relative cultivation of one's sensitivity, represented by interpersonal literacy as well as kindness or affection. Means of literacy—handwriting or reading faces—indicate levels of achievement of that sensitivity, but, as Jude learns, education itself is not salve enough, and no book learning can account for the individual sitting across the dinner table from you.

CHAPTER FOUR

1. The catalogue at the Freer Gallery lists the title as *The Miser* (F1898.310), though the provenance of this title is murky, and it is possible, if not likely, that Whistler himself did not name the piece, especially as the title specifies the content in a way that is atypical of Whistler.

2. "Much of his work came to be anchored within restricted collections, with all the difficulties that ensured for the distant public to see the range of his work [. . .]. Published catalogues of his work were limited to those of his etchings (in 1910) and lithographs (in 1914) compiled by his much-forgiving friend E. G. Kennedy; a catalogue of his paintings did not appear until 1980, and the ink has only just dried on the catalogue of his works on paper, published in 1995. All this has meant that, except for a continuing appreciation of Whistler's graphic art, Whistler's fame has rested largely on his notoriety." Nigel Thorp, "The Butterfly Takes Flight: A Whistler Revival Is Launched," *Archives of American Art Journal* 34, no. 3 (1994): 16–25; 17.

3. Monica Kjellman-Chapin, "Anxious (Dis)figuration: Ingres in Whistler's *Little Blue Girl*," *Art History* 27, no. 1 (January 2004): 34.

4. Linda Merrill offers a delightfully brief summary of the events in her extensively researched history of the trial, *A Pot of Paint: Aesthetics on Trial in Whistler v. Ruskin* (Washington, DC: Smithsonian Institution Press, 1992). "In 1877, having seen several paintings by James McNeill Whistler at the new Grosvenor Gallery in London, John Ruskin condemned *Nocturne in Black and Gold: The Falling Rocket* in a periodical of limited circulation called *Fors Clavigera*. 'I have seen, and heard, much of Cockney impudence before now,' Ruskin wrote, 'but never expected to hear a coxcomb ask two hundred guineas for flinging a pot of paint in the public's face.' Whistler sued the critic for libel, claiming substantial damages, and the case

went to court in November 1878; Ruskin himself was ill and psychologically unfit to appear. After two days of evidence from the plaintiff and several witnesses, the jury declared a verdict in Whistler's favor, but awarded him only a farthing in damages." Merrill, 1.

5. Tim Barringer, "Aestheticism and the Victorian Present: Response," *Victorian Studies* 51, no. 3 (Spring 2009): 455.

6. Whistler appears in nearly every chapter of Lionel Lambourne's lovely *The Aesthetic Movement,* garnering two chapters devoted to him or his works: "A Dissonance in Gold and Silver" and "Whistler and Ruskin: 1878 Watershed of the Aesthetic Movement and Its Aftermath" (London: Phaidon, 1996).

7. Elizabeth Prettejohn, *Art for Art's Sake* (New Haven, CT: Yale University Press, 2007), 167.

8. Elizabeth Prettejohn, *Beauty and Art* (Oxford: Oxford University Press, 2005), 142.

9. Teukolsky points to Whistler's formal emphasis and especially his use of synaesthesia as indication of his Modernist proclivities, noting that his "modernist doctrine" is "epitomized in his musical titles" (155). Teukolsky does not overlook Whistler's French connection entirely, and suggests that his use of musical titles and organizing ideas was inspired by mid-century *symboliste* poetry; and though she associates Whistler's later painting with the work of the French *impressionistes,* his Realist roots do not figure in her analysis. *The Literate Eye* (Oxford: Oxford University Press, 2009).

10. Michael Fried, "The Generation of 1863," in *Manet's Modernism: Or, the Face of Painting in the 1860s* (Chicago: University of Chicago Press, 1996). Fried cannot resist narrativizing Whistler's work. In his analysis of Whistler's 1865–66 *The Artist in His Studio,* the author employs parenthetical suggestions with direct narrative statements to describe the scene: "Behind the painter and seemingly unaware of what he is doing, two women are conversing: one, standing, in a light robe (she has perhaps just been posing for the painter), the other, seated, in a white frock (it's possible she too is a model, but the impression we get is that she is a visitor). The implicit narrative of the picture therefore reads as follows: . . . " (392).

11. James McNeill Whistler to Henri Fantin-Latour, date uncertain (September 1867 or 1868). *Correspondence of James McNeill Whistler,* On-line Edition, edited by Margaret F. MacDonald, Patricia de Montfort, and Nigel Thorp, University of Glasgow, http://www.whistler.arts.gla.ac.uk/correspondence/people/display/?cid=8045&nameid=Courbet_G&sr=0&rs=9&surname=courbet&firstname=.

12. Norman Bryson, *Vision and Painting: The Logic of the Gaze* (New Haven, CT: Yale University Press, 1983), 6.

13. NB: "The history of art is more than a succession of stylistic and iconographic conventions modified by occasional 'comparisons' with perceived reality"; "But important though it might be, fidelity to visual reality was only one aspect of the Realist enterprise; and it would be erroneous to base our conception of so complex a movement on only one of its features: verisimilitude." Linda Nochlin, *Realism* (Middlesex, England: Penguin, 1971), 17, 22–23.

14. Prettejohn, *Art for Art's Sake,* 194.

15. Christopher Benfey, "The Undecider: Bonnard at the Met," *Slate,* http://www.slate.com/id/2210658/(accessed February 13, 2009).

16. Francis Frascina, Nigel Blake, Briony Fer, Tamar Garb, and Charles Harrison, *Modernity and Modernism: French Painting in the Nineteenth Century* (New Haven,

CT: Yale University Press, 1993), 72.

17. Clark: "He has given us, in an almost schematic form, the constituents of a particular ritual, but not their unison [. . .] It is not exactly an image of disbelief, more of collective distraction; not exactly indifference, more inattention; not exactly, except in a few of the women's faces, the marks of grief or the abstraction of mourning, more the careful, ambiguous blankness of a public face." T. J. Clark, *Image of the People: Gustave Courbet and the 1848 Revolution* (London: Thames and Hudson, 1973), 81.

18. The community gathered for Thias Bede's funeral in *Adam Bede* forms a nice complement to the community gathered in Courbet's *Burial at Ornans*.

19. "Are they mother and daughter? The woman is Victorine Meurent, Manet's often used model, and the girl is purportedly the daughter of Manet's neighbor; in short, no" (National Gallery of Art, http://www.nga.gov/feature/manet/intro. shtm, accessed December 19, 2008). In this friendly introduction to Manet's oeuvre through *Chemin de Fer*, the text repeatedly refers to Manet's uniting of high and low, wealthy and poor, dandy and ragpicker, as an indication of his modern impulse and his embrace of the Paris of that day. One risk of such readings is that they tend to blur the disconnection of such scenes. The gentleman may walk across the same bridge as the workman (as in Caillebotte's *Le Pont de l'Europe*, 1877), but shared space does not ensure communality.

20. Nancy Locke, *Manet and the Family Romance* (Princeton, NJ: Princeton University Press, 2003), 97.

21. T. J. Clark, *The Painting of Modern Life* (Princeton, NJ: Princeton University Press, 1984), 146.

22. Manet did meet constantly with a critical reaction that was less than approving and often hostile; he remained befuddled by this response. Those paintings that caused the most furor—*Déjeuner sur l'herbe* and *Olympia*—both feature a kind of triangulation of gazes, wherein the paintings' subjects do not look at each other, but instead cross gazes. They have neither the voyeuristic security of an image in which the subjects are completely unaware of the viewer's gaze nor the ease of a conventional image that is oriented toward the viewer, even if not directly responding to him. But it is clear that critical response then, as now, insisted on reading *into* his paintings. Written in the 1990s, Michael Fried's astute analyses of Manet's works still depend on this reaching beyond the image. Fried argues that Manet's incorporation of visual allusions situates his work within a global art-historical context while also asserting the innate French quality of his artistry. In addition to this interpainting relationship, some argue that Manet's work depends on the assumption that his works enter a knowledgeable community; that is, finding the paintings meaningful depends on placing them in an art-historical context. As Fried suggests, that criticism and art-historical writing on Manet's work do not adequately *read* the allusions in his works amounts to misreading his intentions. Fried, *Manet's Modernism*, 4. These trends in painting and the art-historical constructions that insist on interpretation lead to the situation against which Whistler railed so strongly (and his response came even before art historians would considerably fortify their devotion to the strategy); such tendencies were contemporary with Whistler and have continued to flourish since that time.

23. One must imagine that Whistler fully anticipated his audience connecting his *White Girl* with Wilkie Collins's immensely popular *The Woman in White*, which would still have been fresh in their collective imagination. NB: Robin Spen-

cer, "Whistler's 'The White Girl': Painting, Poetry, and Meaning," *The Burlington Magazine* 140, no. 1142 (May 1998): 300–311; and Aileen Tsui's "The Phantasm of Aesthetic Autonomy in Whistler's Work: Titling *The White Girl*," *Art History* 29, no. 3 (June 2006): 444–75.

24. Spencer, "Whistler's 'The White Girl,'" 300. Rachel Teukolsky also writes on *The White Girl*, situating the image within the narrative and iconic tradition of other "white girls" of the period—a strongly British tradition. "White Girls: Avant-Gardism and Advertising after 1860," *Victorian Studies* 51, no. 3 (Spring 2009): 422–37.

25. Pamela Fletcher, "'To wipe a manly tear': The Aesthetics of Emotion in Victorian Narrative Painting," *Victorian Studies* 51, no. 3 (Spring 2009): 458.

26. James McNeill Whistler, *Ten O'Clock* (London: Chatto and Windus, 1888), 9.

27. Sarah Burns, "Review of *A Pot of Paint: Aestheticism on Trial in Whistler v. Ruskin* by Linda Merrill," *Winterthur Portfolio* 28, no. 1 (Spring 1993): 105.

28. Compare with T. J. Clark's reading of Manet's *Olympia* above, wherein the decorative additions—the cat, the necklace, and so forth—are simply "lures" that work against a narrative. Here, those similar details are actually constitutive of that narrative, and nearly literal in their meaning.

29. John Ruskin, vol. 14 of *The Works of John Ruskin* (London: George Allen, 1904), 166. Also quoted in gallery notes, which add, "Ruskin's comments show that audiences were expected to 'read' pictures like novels." http://www.tate.org.uk/servlet/ViewWork?cgroupid=999999961&workid=4092&searchid=9658&currow=4&maxrows=5 (accessed March 14, 2008).

30. *Ten O'Clock*, 17.

31. Despite Whistler's clearly articulated views on these points, some still insist on pressing the point. Dan Nadaner, writing about the potentially fruitful pedagogical engagement of visual and textual intersections, suggests that both Whistler *and* Turner were painters who "write their images." "On Relatedness between the Arts: Crossovers between Painting and Poetry," *Journal of Aesthetic Education* 27, no. 1 (Spring 1993): 31–39.

32. David Craven, "Ruskin vs. Whistler: The Case against Capitalist Art," *Art Journal* 37, no. 2 (Winter 1977–78): 142.

33. Elizabeth Helsinger, *Ruskin and the Art of the Beholder* (Cambridge, MA: Harvard University Press, 1982), 190.

34. Ibid., 192.

35. From the *Pall Mall Gazette*, February 21, 1885. Reprinted in *Wilde v. Whistler, Being an Acrimonious Correspondence on Art between Oscar Wilde and James McNeill Whistler* (London: Privately printed, 1906), 6.

36. Ibid., 8.

37. Kathleen Pyne, "Whistler and the Politics of the Urban Picturesque," *American Art* 8, no. 3/4 (Summer-Autumn 1994): 61. That's "aestheticism," not "Aestheticism."

38. Roy McMullen, *Victorian Outsider: A Biography of J. A. M. Whistler* (New York: E. P. Dutton, 1973), 82.

39. Monica Kjellman-Chapin, "Anxious (Dis)Figuration," 34.

40. C. Stocks, "Review of *Whistler's Mother*," *Modern Painters* 16, no. 3 (Autumn 2003): 136.

41. See Manet's *Mme. Manet at the Piano* (1868) and Degas's *M. and Mme. Manet at the Piano* (1868–69) for reworkings of this element of Whistler's work.

42. White was considered appropriate for young middle-class children in mourning. Cf. Judith Flanders, *Inside the Victorian Home* (New York: W. W. Norton and Company, 2004), 371–72.

43. "With the exception of photographs." Jonathan Crary, *Techniques of the Observer* (Cambridge, MA: MIT University Press, 1992), 116. Crary goes on to link the development of stereoscopic imagery to some of the strategies of depiction used by Realist painters: "A range of nineteenth-century painting also manifests some of these features of stereoscopic imagery. [. . .] I am suggesting that *both* the 'realism' of the stereoscope and the 'experiments' of certain painters were equally bound up in a much broader transformation of the observer that allowed the emergence of this new optically constructed space." Ibid., 126.

44. This most important aspect of the painting is merely glossed in the Taft's gallery notes, which suggest that her blurred face might indicate motion (as if it were a photograph).

45. "The new canvas again utilized the music room [. . .]. The impact is curious, for the massively black Miss Boot is almost surreal amidst the chintz-curtained and picture-hung fussiness of the quiet nineteenth-century room." Stanley Weintraub, *Whistler: A Biography* (New York: E. P. Dutton, 1974), 67. "Nearly a third of the area is occupied by the cream, green, and deep pink chintz drapery." McMullen, *Victorian Outsider*, 88. "The focus of the house was the music room, where filtered sunlight and shaded gaslight managed to unify maroon carpeting, green-tinted walls, pictures in heavy gold frames, a large mirror, a grand piano, and a profusion of chintz drapery, cream colored with a floral pattern in green and deep pink." McMullen, 81.

46. Manet, too, would capitalize on the claustrophobic setting of an image. His *Le Balcon* of 1868 reveals a similar setting of three figures, each facing a different direction, each contained in a small, cluttered space, and all appearing as if they were plucked from three disparate canvases and collaged onto this balcony by the artist. Whistler also painted a balcony scene, similarly cluttered; *The Balcony* (1864–70) is seen from the inside, and the sitters are united in their *japonisme* trappings, but it is otherwise quite similar to Manet's.

47. Writes Florence Nightingale Levy in *Paintings in Oil and Pastel by James Whistler*, "The first title of the picture was The Morning Call" (New York: The Gilliss Press, 1910), 1. Weintraub writes that the original title was *The Music Room*. *Whistler*, vii. The title is satirized in *Punch*: a "Matron in Search of a Subject" likes the painting, thinking it pretty, and asking her daughter to see what it is called so as to clear up her confusion as to what it is about, what it depicts: "Do see what it's called. '*The Morning Canter*,' or '*Back from the Row*'—something of that kind, I *expect* it would be." When her daughter replies that "all it says is, '*A Harmony in Green and Rose*,'" her mother retorts disappointedly, "Now, why can't he give it some *sensible* name, instead of taking away all one's interest!" "Wrestling with Whistlers," *Punch* 102 (April 16, 1892): 181.

48. "There may be a narrative content once one brings to mind Whistler's family relations. It then turns out that the most important figure in terms of visual presence is the least important one, i.e., Miss Boott [*sic*], a long-standing family acquaintance but without any apparent emotional ties. . . ." Gisela Schmidt, "I see, I see, said the Blind Man," *Journal of Visual Art Practice* 4, no. 2/3 (2005): 151–65.

49. When Whistler sought to cancel a plate that had reached the end of its

printing run, he covered it with cross-hatchings that are remarkably similar to the markings in these dockland scenes.

50. "These three figures are sitting on the balcony of the Angel Inn in London's docklands. The woman is a prostitute, and is apparently taunting the sailor on the right; the man in the middle may be a pimp." "Thames Views: Wapping," *Tate Britain*, http://www.tate.org.uk/britain/exhibitions/turnerwhistlermonet/ thamesviews/wapping.htm (accessed December 17, 2009).

"[Whistler's] *Wapping* was painted at a 'dive,' the Angel Inn, Cherry Gardens, Rotherhithe. Its indecency was toned down, after a friend warned Whistler that the extreme décolletage of the prostitute (a 'jolly gal' with a 'superlatively whorish air,' as Whistler described her, modeled on his fiery mistress, Jo Hiffernan) would prevent the painting's acceptance by the R.A. jury." Alan Robinson, "Aesthetes, Impressionists, and Parvenus: Some Early Trials of Modern Painting in London," in *Aspects of Modernism*, eds. Andreas Fischer, Martine Heusser, and Thomas Hermann (Tübingen: Gunter Narr Verlag, 1997), 24.

51. Whistler, *Ten O'Clock*, 9. Emphasis in the original.

CONCLUSION

1. Johann Wolfgang von Goethe, *The Sorrows of Young Werther*, trans. R. Dillon Boylan (Boston: F. A. Nicolls and Co, 1902).

2. George Eliot, *Middlemarch* (London: Penguin, 1994), 3, 4.

Ablow, Rachel. *The Marriage of Minds: Reading Sympathy in the Victorian Marriage Plot.* Stanford, CA: Stanford University Press, 2007.

Albrecht, T'homas. "Sympathy and Telepathy: The Problems of Ethics in George Eliot's *The Lifted Veil.*" *ELH* 73, no. 2 (2006): 437–63.

Alter, Robert. "The Demons of History in Dickens' *Tale.*" *NOVEL: A Forum on Fiction* 2, no. 2 (Winter 1969): 135–42.

Anderson, Amanda. *The Powers of Distance: Cosmopolitanism and the Cultivation of Detachment.* Princeton, NJ: Princeton University Press, 2001.

————. *Tainted Souls and Painted Faces: The Rhetoric of Fallenness in Victorian Culture.* Ithaca, NY: Cornell University Press, 1993.

Argyros, Ellen. *"Without Any Check of Proud Reserve": Sympathy and Its Limits in George Eliot's Novels.* Studies in Nineteenth-Century British Literature. New York: Peter Lang, 1999.

Attridge, Derek. "Innovation, Literature, Ethics: Relating to the Other." *PMLA* 114, no. 1 (January 1999): 20–31.

Auerbach, Erich. *Mimesis.* Princeton, NJ: Princeton University Press, 1953.

Auerbach, Nina. "The Rise of the Fallen Woman." *Nineteenth-Century Fiction* 35, no. 1 (1980): 29–53.

Balzac, Honoré de. *La Peau du chagrin.* In *Oeuvres complètes.* Paris: Editions de Delta, 1976.

————. *Le Père Goriot.* Paris: Pocket Books, 1989.

Barringer, Tim. "Aestheticism and the Victorian Present: Response." *Victorian Studies* 51, no. 3 (Spring 2009): 451–56.

————. "Images of Otherness and the Visual Production of Difference: Race and Labour in Illustrated Texts, 1850–1865." In *The Victorians and Race,* ed. Shearer West, 34–52. Brookfield, VT: Ashgate Press, 1996.

Barthes, Roland. "The Man-Eater." In *Critical Essays on Émile Zola,* ed. David Baguley, 93. Boston: G. K. Hall and Co., 1955.

Bellos, David. *Balzac Criticism in France 1830–1900.* London: Clarendon Press, 1976.

Bellringer, Alan. *George Eliot.* New York: St. Martin's, 1993.

Benfey, Christopher. "The Undecider: Bonnard at the Met." *Slate,* February 11, 2009. http://www.slate.com/id/2210658.

Blake, Kathleen. "Pure Tess: Hardy on Knowing a Woman." *Studies in English*

Literature: 1500–1900 22, no. 4 (Autumn 1982): 689–705.

_____. "Sue Bridehead, 'Woman of the Feminist Movement.'" *Studies in English Literature* 18, no. 4 (Autumn 1978): 703–26.

Blind, Mathilde. *George Eliot*. London: W. H. Allen and Co., 1883.

Bodenheimer, Rosemarie. *Knowing Dickens*. Ithaca, NY: Cornell University Press, 2007.

Bonaparte, Felicia. *Will and Destiny; Morality and Tragedy in George Eliot's Novels*. New York: New York University Press, 1975.

Booth, Wayne. *The Company We Keep: An Ethics of Fiction*. Berkeley: University of California Press, 1988.

Boyd, Michael. *The Reflexive Novel*. Lewisburg, PA: Bucknell University Press, 1983.

Brooks, Peter. *Reading for the Plot: Design and Intention in Narrative*. Cambridge, MA: Harvard University Press, 1992.

_____. *Realist Visions*. New Haven, CT: Yale University Press, 2005.

Bryson, Norman. *Vision and Painting: The Logic of the Gaze*. New Haven, CT: Yale University Press, 1983.

Burns, Sarah. "Review of *A Pot of Paint: Aestheticism on Trial in Whistler v. Ruskin*, by Linda Merrill." *Winterthur Portfolio* 28, no. 1 (Spring 1993): 105–8.

Byrd, Max. "Reading in *Great Expectations*." *PMLA* 91, no. 2 (March 1976): 259–65.

Carroll, David. *George Eliot and the Conflict of Interpretations*. Cambridge: Cambridge University Press, 1992.

_____, ed. *George Eliot: The Critical Heritage*. New York: Barnes and Noble, 1971.

Clark, T. J. *Image of the People: Gustave Courbet and the 1848 Revolution*. London: Thames and Hudson, 1973.

_____. *The Painting of Modern Life*. Princeton, NJ: Princeton University Press, 1984.

Cobley, Paul. *Narrative*. London: Routledge, 2001.

Cooke, George Willis. *George Eliot: A Critical Study of Her Life, Writings and Philosophy*. Boston: J. R. Osgood, 1884.

Cowles, David. "Methods of Inquiry, Modes of Evidence: Perception, Self-Deception, and Truth in *Bleak House*." *The Dickensian* 87, no. 425 (Autumn 1991): 153–62.

Cox, R. G. *Thomas Hardy: The Critical Heritage*. London: Routledge, 1970.

Crary, Jonathan. *Techniques of the Observer*. Cambridge, MA: MIT University Press, 1992.

Craven, David. "Ruskin vs. Whistler: The Case against Capitalist Art." *Art Journal* 37, no. 2 (Winter 1977–78): 139–43.

Cross, John Walter. *George Eliot's Life as Related in Her Letters and Journals*, vols.1 and 2. London: Blackwood, 1885.

Davis, W. Eugene. "*Tess of the d'Urbervilles:* Some Ambiguities about a Pure Woman." *Nineteenth-Century Fiction* 22, no. 4 (March 1968): 397–401.

Dever, Carolyn M. "Broken Mirror, Broken Words: Autobiography, Prosopopeia and the Dead Mother in *Bleak House*." *Studies in the Novel* 27, no. 1 (Spring 1995): 42–66.

DiBattista, Maria. *First Love: The Affections of Modern Fiction*. Chicago: University of Chicago Press, 1991.

Dickens, Charles. *Bleak House*. London: Penguin, 2003.

_____. *David Copperfield*. London: Penguin, 2004.

_____. *Great Expectations*. London, Penguin, 2002.

_____. *Oliver Twist*. London: Penguin, 1985.

_____. *A Tale of Two Cities*. London: Penguin, 2003.

Eliot, George. *Adam Bede*. London: Penguin, 2008.

_____. *The Lifted Veil*. London: Penguin, 2001.

_____. *Middlemarch*. London: Penguin, 1994.

_____. *Selected Essays, Poems, and Other Writings*. London: Penguin, 1990.

Feltes, N. N. "Phrenology: From Lewes to George Eliot." *Studies in the Literary Imagination* 1, no. 1 (April 1968): 13–22.

Fenstermaker, John. "Language Abuse in *Bleak House:* The First Monthly Installment." In *Victorian Literature and Society*, ed. James Kincaid, 240–257. Columbus: The Ohio State University Press, 1984.

Flanders, Judith. *Inside the Victorian Home*. New York: W. W. Norton and Company, 2004.

Fletcher, Pamela. "'To wipe a manly tear': The Aesthetics of Emotion in Victorian Narrative Painting." *Victorian Studies* 51, no. 3 (Spring 2009): 457–69.

Flint, Kate. "Blood, Bodies, and *The Lifted Veil*." *Nineteenth-Century Literature* 51, no. 4 (March 1997): 455–73.

Forster, E. M. *Aspects of the Novel*. New York: Harvest Books, 1956.

Forster, John. *The Life of Charles Dickens*. London: Lippincott and Co., 1874.

Franklin, Michael J. "'Market-Faces' and Market Forces: [Corn-]Factors in the Moral Economy of Casterbridge." *Review of English Studies* 59 (June 2008): 426–48.

Frascina, Francis, Nigel Blake, Briony Fer, Tamar Garb, and Charles Harrison. *Modernity and Modernism: French Painting in the Nineteenth Century*. New Haven, CT: Yale University Press, 1993.

Fried, Michael. *Manet's Modernism, or the Face of Painting in the 1860s*. Chicago: University of Chicago Press, 1996.

Furst, Lilian R. *All Is True: The Claims and Strategies of Realist Fiction*. Durham, NC: Duke University Press, 1995.

Gagnier, Regenia. "Review of *Rule of Darkness: British Literature and Imperialism, 1830–1914* by Patrick Brantlinger." *Modern Philology* 87, no. 3 (February 1990): 316–19.

Gallagher, Catherine. *Nobody's Story: The Vanishing Acts of Women Writers in the Marketplace 1670–1820*. Berkeley: University of California Press, 1995.

Gallatin, A. E. *Whistler: Notes and Footnotes*. New York: The Collector and Art Critic Company, 1907.

Gill, Stephen. Introduction to *Adam Bede*, by George Eliot, ix–xxxvii. London: Penguin, 1980.

Goethe, Johann Wolfgang von. *The Sorrows of Young Werther*. Trans. R. Dillon Boylan. Boston: F. A. Nicolls and Co, 1902.

Gombrich, Ernst. *Art and Illusion*. London: Phaidon, 1977.

Goode, John. *Thomas Hardy: The Offensive Truth*. Oxford: Basil Blackwell, 1988.

Gordon, Jan B. "Origins, History, and the Reconstitution of Family: Tess' Journey." *ELH* 43, no. 3 (Autumn 1976): 366–88.

Graver, Suzanne. *George Eliot and Community: A Study in Social Theory and Fictional Form*. Berkeley, CA: University of California Press, 1984.

Greiner, Rae. "Sympathy Time: Adam Smith, George Eliot, and the Realist Novel." *Narrative* 17, no. 3 (October 2009): 291–311.

Hale, Dorothy. *Social Formalism: The Novel in Theory from Henry James to the Present.* Stanford, CA: Stanford University Press, 1998.

Haney, David P. "Aesthetics and Ethics in Gadamer, Levinas, and Romanticism: Problems of Phronesis and Teche." *PMLA* 114, no. 1 (January 1999): 32–45.

Hardy, Barbara. *Rituals: Feelings in the Novels of George Eliot.* London: University of Swansea Press, 1973.

_____. "Towards a Poetics of Fiction: 3) An Approach through Narrative." *Novel: A Forum on Fiction* 2, no. 1 (Autumn 1968): 5–14.

Hardy, Thomas. *Collected Letters of Thomas Hardy,* vol. 2, *1893–1901,* ed. Richard Little Purdy and Michael Millgate. London: Clarendon Press, 1980.

_____. *Far from the Madding Crowd.* London: Penguin, 2003.

_____. *Jude the Obscure.* London: Penguin, 1998.

_____. *The Mayor of Casterbridge.* London: Penguin, 2003.

_____. *The Pursuit of the Well-Beloved* and *The Well-Beloved.* London: Penguin, 1998.

_____. *Tess of the d'Urbervilles.* London: Penguin, 2003.

_____. *The Woodlanders.* London: Penguin, 1998.

Harrison, Mary-Catherine. "The Paradox of Fiction and the Ethics of Empathy: Reconceiving Dickens's Realism." *Narrative* 16, no. 3 (October 2008): 256–78.

Hawkins, Desmond. *Thomas Hardy.* London: A. Barker, 1950.

Helsinger, Elizabeth K. *Ruskin and the Art of the Beholder.* Cambridge, MA: Harvard University Press, 1982.

Henry, Nancy. *George Eliot and the British Empire.* Cambridge: Cambridge University Press, 2000.

Hertz, Neil. *George Eliot's Pulse.* Palo Alto, CA: Stanford University Press, 2003.

Higonnet, Margaret. Introduction to *Tess of the d'Urbervilles* by Thomas Hardy. London: Penguin, 1998.

Hinton, Laura. *The Perverse Gaze of Sympathy: Sadomasochistic Sentiments from "Clarissa" to "Rescue 911."* New York: State University of New York Press, 1999.

Hough, Graham. "Language and Reality in *Bleak House.*" In *Realism in European Literature,* ed. Nicholas Boyle and Martin Swales, 50–67. Cambridge: Cambridge University Press, 1986.

Hume, David. *A Treatise of Human Nature.* London: John Noon, 1886.

Humphreys, Camilla. "Dickens's Use of Letters in *Bleak House.*" *Dickens Quarterly* 6, no. 2 (June 1989): 53–60.

Huntley, Dana. "Greatest Painting in Britain." *British Heritage* 26, no. 6 (January 2006): 8.

Jaffe, Audrey. *Scenes of Sympathy: Identity and Representation in Victorian Fiction.* Ithaca, NY: Cornell University Press, 2000.

Keen, Suzanne. *Empathy and the Novel.* Princeton, NJ: Princeton University Press, 2007.

Keller, Evelyn Fox. *Reflections on Gender and Science.* New Haven, CT: Yale University Press, 1986.

Kjellman-Chapin, Monica. "Anxious (Dis)figuration: Ingres in Whistler's *Little Blue Girl.*" *Art History* 27, no. 1 (January 2004): 34–61.

Kucich, John. *The Power of Lies: Transgression in Victorian Literature.* Ithaca, NY: Cornell University Press, 1994.

Laird, J. T. "New Light on the Evolution of *Tess of the d'Urbervilles.*" *The Review of*

English Studies 31, no. 124 (November 1980): 414–35.

Lambourne, Lionel. *The Aesthetic Movement.* London: Phaidon 1996.

Langland, Elizabeth. "A Perspective of One's Own: Thomas Hardy and the Elusive Sue Bridehead." *Studies in the Novel* 12, no. 1 (Spring 1980): 12–30.

Larson, Jil. *Ethics and Narrative in the English Novel, 1880–1914.* Cambridge: Cambridge University Press, 2001.

Leavis, Q. D. "How We Must Read *Great Expectations.*" In *Dickens the Novelist*, 277–331. London: Pantheon, 1970.

Lecker, Barbara. "The Split Characters of Charles Dickens." *Studies in English Literature, 1500–1900* 19, no. 4 (Autumn 1979): 689–704.

Levinas, Emmanuel. "The Other in Proust." In *The Levinas Reader*, ed. Seán Hand, 160–65. London: Blackwell, 1989.

_____. *Otherwise than Being.* Pittsburgh, PA: Duquesne University Press, 1969.

_____. *Outside the Subject.* Trans. Michael Smith. London: The Athlone Press, 1993.

_____. "The Proximity of the Other." In *Is It Righteous to Be? Interviews with Emmanuel Levinas*, ed. Jill Robbins, 211–18. Stanford, CA: Stanford University Press, 2001.

_____. "Reality and Its Shadow." In *The Levinas Reader*, ed. Seán Hand, 129–43. London: Blackwell, 1989.

_____. *Time and the Others.* Trans. Richard A. Cohen. Pittsburgh, PA: Duquesne University Press, 1987.

_____. *Totality and Infinity: An Essay on Exteriority.* Pittsburgh, PA: Duquesne University Press, 1969.

Levine, Caroline. *The Serious Pleasures of Suspense: Victorian Realism and Narrative Doubt.* Charlottesville: University of Virginia Press, 2003.

Levine, George. *Dying to Know: Scientific Epistemology and Narrative in Victorian England.* Chicago: University of Chicago Press, 2002.

_____. "Looking for the Real." Introduction to *Realism and Representation: Essays on the Problem of Realism in Relation to Science, Literature, and Culture*, ed. George Levine, 3–26. Madison: University of Wisconsin Press, 1993.

_____. *The Realistic Imagination: English Fiction from Frankenstein to Lady Chatterley.* Chicago: University of Chicago Press, 1981.

Levy, Florence Nightingale. *Paintings in Oil and Pastel by James Whistler.* New York: The Gilliss Press, 1910.

Locke, Nancy. *Manet and the Family Romance.* Princeton, NJ: Princeton University Press, 2003.

Lowe, Brigid. *Victorian Fiction and the Insights of Sympathy.* London: Anthem Press, 2007.

MacDonald, Margaret F. *James McNeill Whistler: Drawings, Pastels and Watercolours: A Catalogue Raisonné.* New Haven, CT: Yale University Press, 1995.

Marck, Nancy Ann. "Narrative Transference and Female Narcissism: The Social Message of *Adam Bede.*" *Studies in the Novel* 35, no. 4 (Winter 2003): 447–69.

Marshall, David. *The Surprising Effects of Sympathy.* Chicago: University of Chicago Press, 1988.

McMullen, Roy. *Victorian Outsider: A Biography of J. A. M. Whistler.* New York: E. P. Dutton, 1973.

Mensch, James Richard. *Hiddenness and Alterity: Philosophical and Literary Sightings of the Unseen.* Pittsburgh, PA: Duquesne University Press, 2005.

Merrill, Linda. *A Pot of Paint: Aesthetics on Trial in Whistler v. Ruskin.* Washington, DC: Smithsonian Institution Press, 1992.

Mill, John Stuart. *On Liberty and other Essays.* Ed. John Gray. Oxford: Oxford University Press, 1991.

Miller, Andrew. *The Burdens of Perfection: On Ethics and Reading in Nineteenth-Century British Literature.* Ithaca, NY: Cornell University Press, 2008.

Miller, Joseph Hillis. "Is Literary Theory a Science?" In *Realism and Representation,* ed. George Levine, 155–68. Madison: University of Wisconsin Press: 1993.

————. *Others.* Princeton, NJ: Princeton University Press, 2001.

————. *Thomas Hardy, Distance and Desire.* Cambridge, MA: Harvard University Press, 1970.

————. *Victorian Subjects.* Durham, NC: Duke University Press, 1991.

Mitchell, Judith. "George Eliot and the Problematic of Female Beauty." *Modern Language Studies* 20, no. 3 (Summer 1990): 14–28.

Mitchell, Rebecca N. "Learning to Read: Interpersonal Literacy in *Adam Bede.*" *Papers on Language and Literature* 44, no. 2 (Spring 2008): 145–67.

Mitchell, W. J. T. *What Do Pictures Want? The Lives and Loves of Images.* Chicago: University of Chicago Press, 2005.

Moretti, Franco. "Serious Century." In *History, Geography, and Culture,* vol. 1 of *The Novel,* ed. Franco Moretti, 364–400. Princeton, NJ: Princeton University Press, 2006.

Morgan, H. Cliff. "The Schools of the Royal Academy." *British Journal of Educational Studies* 21, no. 1 (February 1973): 88–103.

Morgan, Monique. "Conviction in Writing: Crime, Confession, and the Written Word in *Great Expectations.*" *Dickens Study Annual* 33 (2003): 87–108.

Nadaner, Dan. "On Relatedness between the Arts: Crossovers between Painting and Poetry." *Journal of Aesthetic Education* 27, no. 1 (Spring 1993): 31–39.

Newton, Adam Zachary. *Narrative Ethics.* Cambridge, MA: Harvard University Press, 1995.

Nochlin, Linda. *Realism.* Middlesex, England: Penguin, 1971.

Nussbaum, Martha. *Love's Knowledge: Essays on Philosophy and Literature.* New York: Oxford University Press, 1990.

Paris, Bernard. *Rereading George Eliot: Changing Responses to Her Experiments in Life.* Albany: State University of New York Press, 2003.

Pliny. *Natural History.* London: Bell and Sons, 1898.

Pound, Ezra. "Ezra Pound on Turner, 1909." *Tate Britain: Turner Online.* http://www.tate.org.uk/britain/turner/pound.htm.

Prettejohn, Elizabeth. *Art for Art's Sake.* New Haven, CT: Yale University Press, 2007.

————. *Beauty and Art.* Oxford: Oxford University Press, 2005.

Putnam, Hilary. *Realism with a Human Face.* Cambridge, MA: Harvard University Press, 1990.

Pyne, Kathleen. "Whistler and the Politics of the Urban Picturesque." *American Art* 8, no. 3/4 (Summer–Autumn 1994): 61–77.

"Review of *Perspective: Its Principle and Practice.*" *The Art-Journal* 7 (1 June 1850): 202.

Robbins, Bruce. "Telescopic Philanthropy." In *Nation and Narration,* ed. Homi K. Bhabha, 213–30. New York: Routledge, 1990.

Robinson, Alan. "Aesthetes, Impressionists, and Parvenus: Some Early Trials of Modern Painting in London." In *Aspects of Modernism,* ed. Andreas Fischer, Martin Heusser, and Thomas Hermann, 19–32. Tübingen: Gunet Narr Verlag, 1997.

Root, Winthrop Hegeman. *German Criticism of Zola, 1875–1893.* New York: Columbia University Press, 1931.

Roy, Paula. "Agent or Victim: Thomas Hardy's *Tess of the d'Urbervilles.*" In *Women in Literature: Reading through the Lens of Gender,* ed. Jerilyn Fisher and Ellen S. Silber, 277–79. Westport, CT: Greenwood Publishing Group, 2003.

Ruskin, John. "The Fighting Téméraire Tugged to Her Last Berth to Be Broken Up (1838)." In *Great Pictures as Seen and Described by Famous Writers,* ed. Esther Singleton. 306–12. London: Dodd, Mead and Co., 1899.

_____. *The Works of John Ruskin.* London: George Allen, 1905.

Saint-Amour, Paul. "'Christmas Yet to Come': Hospitality, Futurity, the *Carol,* and 'The Dead'" *Representations* 98 (Spring 2007): 93–117.

Schehr, Lawrence. *Figures of Alterity: French Realism and Its Others.* Palo Alto, CA: Stanford University Press, 2003.

Schmidt, Gisela. "I see, I see, said the Blind Man." *Journal of Visual Art Practice* 4, no. 2/3 (2005): 151–65.

Schor, Hilary. *Dickens and the Daughter of the House.* Cambridge: Cambridge University Press, 1999.

Shires, Linda. "'And I Was Unaware': The Unknowing Omniscience of Hardy's Narrators." In *Thomas Hardy: Texts and Contexts,* ed. Phillip Mallett, 31–48. London: Palgrave Macmillan, 2002.

Shuttleworth, Sally. Introduction to *The Lifted Veil and Brother Jacob,* by George Eliot. London: Penguin, 2001.

Siebers, Tobin. *Morals and Stories.* New York: Columbia University Press, 1992.

Siemerling, Winfried. *Discoveries of the Other: Alterity in the Work of Leonard Cohen, Hubert Aquin, Michael Ondaatje, and Nicole Brossard.* Toronto: University of Toronto Press, 1994.

Silverman, Kaja. "History, Figuration, and Female Subjectivity in *Tess of the d'Urbervilles.*" *Novel: A Forum on Fiction* 18, no. 1 (Autumn 1984): 5–28.

Smith, Adam. *The Theory of Moral Sentiments.* London: Henry G. Bohn, 1853.

Spencer, Robin. "Whistler's 'The White Girl': Painting, Poetry, and Meaning." *The Burlington Magazine* 140, no. 1142 (May 1998): 300–311.

Stewart, Garrett. *The Look of Reading: Book, Painting, and Text.* Chicago: University of Chicago Press, 2006.

Stocks, C. "Review of *Whistler's Mother.*" *Modern Painters* 16, no. 3 (Autumn 2003): 136.

Stone, Donald. "Beauty Running in the World." *Sewanee Review* 107, no. 4 (Fall 1999): 618–25.

Tanner, Tony. "Colour and Movement in Hardy's *Tess of the d'Urbervilles.*" *Critical Quarterly* 10, no. 3 (1968): 219–39.

Tate Gallery. "Past and Present" gallery note. http://www.tate.org.uk/servlet/ViewWork?cgroupid=999999961&workid=4092&searchid=9658&currow=4&maxrows=5.

Teukolsky, Rachel. *The Literate Eye.* Oxford: Oxford University Press, 2009.

_____. "White Girls: Avant-Gardism and Advertising after 1860." *Victorian Studies* 51, no. 3 (Spring 2009): 422–37.

"Thames Views: Wapping," *Tate Britain,* http://www.tate.org.uk/britain/exhibitions/turnerwhistlermonet/thamesviews/wapping.htm.

Thorp, Nigel. "The Butterfly Takes Flight: A Whistler Revival is Launched." *Archives of American Art Journal* 34, no. 3 (1994): 16–25.

Tsui, Aileen. "The Phantasm of Aesthetic Autonomy in Whistler's Work: Titling *The White Girl.*" *Art History* 29, no. 3 (June 2006): 444–75.

Uglow, Jennifer. *George Eliot.* London: Virago, 1987.

Van Zuylan, Marina. *Monomania.* Ithaca, NY: Cornell University Press, 2005.

Vizetelly, Ernest. *Émile Zola, Novelist and Reformer.* London: J. Lane, 1904.

Weinberg, Bernard. *French Realism: The Critical Reaction, 1830–1870.* London: Oxford University Press, 1937.

Weintraub, Stanley. *Whistler: A Biography.* New York: E. P. Dutton, 1974.

Whistler, James Abbott McNeill. *Correspondence of James McNeill Whistler,* On-line Edition, eds. Margaret F. MacDonald, Patricia de Montfort, and Nigel Thorp, University of Glasgow. http://www.whistler.arts.gla.ac.uk/correspondence.

————. *The Gentle Art of Making Enemies.* London: William Heineman, 1892.

————. *Ten O'Clock.* London: Chatto and Windus, 1888.

————. *Wilde v. Whistler, Being an Acrimonious Correspondence on Art between Oscar Wilde and James A. McNeill Whistler.* London: Privately printed, 1906.

————. *Whistler on Art: Selected Letters and Writings of James McNeill Whistler,* ed. Nigel Thorp. Manchester, UK: Fyfield Books, 1994.

Wike, Jonathan. "The World as Text in Hardy's Fiction." *Nineteenth-Century Literature* 47, no. 4 (March 1993): 455–71.

Wilde, Oscar, *The Picture of Dorian Gray.* New York: Norton, 1988.

Williams, D. A., ed. *The Monster in the Mirror.* London: Oxford University Press, 1978.

"Wrestling with Whistlers." *Punch* 102 (April 16, 1892): 181.

Wright, T. R. "From Bumps to Morals: The Phrenological Background to George Eliot's Moral Framework." *The Review of English Studies* 33, no. 129 (February 1982): 34–46.

Yeazell, Ruth Bernard. *Art of the Everyday: Dutch Painting and the Realist Novel.* Princeton, NJ: Princeton University Press, 2008.

Young, Andrew McLaren, Margaret MacDonald, Robin Spencer, and Hamish Miles. *The Paintings of James McNeill Whistler.* New Haven, CT: Yale University Press, 1980.

Young, Kay. "*Middlemarch* and the Problem of Other Minds Heard." *Literature, Interpretation, Theory* 14 (2003): 223–41.

Young, Sandra. "Uneasy Relations: Possibilities for Eloquence in *Bleak House.*" *Dickens Studies Annual* 9 (1981): 67–85.

INDEX

VICTORIAN CRITICAL INTERVENTIONS
Donald E. Hall, Series Editor

Included in this series are provocative, theory-based forays into some of the most heated discussions in Victorian studies today, with the goal of redefining what we both know and do in this field.